THE EXOTIC COLLECTION

VOLUME ONE

TITAN
BOOKS

London

Season 1:
THE RED WAR · 5

Season 2:
THE CURSE OF OSIRIS · 33

Season 3:
WARMIND · 43

Season 4:
FORSAKEN—SEASON OF THE OUTLAW · 55

Season 5:
SEASON OF THE FORGE · 75

Season 6:
SEASON OF THE DRIFTER · 87

Season 7:
SEASON OF OPULENCE · 95

Season 8:
SHADOWKEEP—SEASON OF THE UNDYING · 105

Season 9:
SEASON OF DAWN · 117

Season 10:
SEASON OF THE WORTHY · 123

Season 11:
SEASON OF ARRIVALS · 131

Season 12:
BEYOND LIGHT—SEASON OF THE HUNT · 141

Season 13:
SEASON OF THE CHOSEN · 159

Season 14:
SEASON OF THE SPLICER · 167

Season 15:
SEASON OF THE LOST · 173

Season 1
THE RED WAR

Dominus Ghaul led his Red Legion Cabal on an assault of the Last City. Victorious, he used Cabal technology to ensnare the Traveler and block Guardians' access to the Light.

The Guardian regathered the Vanguard and mounted a counterassault to take back humanity's home. Ghaul's plan to steal the Light backfired, and the Traveler destroyed him.

BOREALIS

Light is a spectrum. Why limit yourself to a single hue?

"Project Borealis's onboard systems contain a pocket energy matrix capable of changing its alignment in a near instant to mimic the spectral frequencies of mapped energy types. The science is groundbreaking, but volatile. We're lucky to have this first, stable model available for active combat use. More will surely come, but for now, the Borealis is the only one of its kind that I trust for real-world application."

"Sounds dangerous."

"If the internal matrix misaligns for any reason during its shift between outputs—damage, wear, a flaw in its production—the resulting feedback could [REDACTED]."

"That bad, huh?"

"If your definition of 'bad' includes the [REDACTED], then, yes, 'bad' begins to describe it."

COLDHEART

The latest Omolon engineering leverages liquid fuel as coolant to keep weapon systems at biting subzero temperatures.

The Golden Age. Our shining history. The height from which we fell. Once, everything we had was borrowed from the past. Since the Collapse, we have struggled to reclaim even a scrap of what our ancestors once took for granted. Over the years, Omolon has perfected the art of salvaging Golden Age technologies and repurposing them into effective Guardian weaponry.

But Coldheart is something new.

We didn't find Coldheart. We didn't adapt it or recycle it. We created it. Its liquid ammo, which doubles as its coolant, is a game changer on its own—never mind Coldheart's first-of-its-kind laser-powered trace vweaponry.

With Coldheart, we at Omolon are saying, we want more than to simply reclaim the Golden Age. We want to surpass it.

D.A.R.C.I.

Thank you for using the Data Analysis, Reconnaissance, and Cooperative Intelligence device. You may call me Darci.

It is a fact generally understood that a Guardian must be searching for an exquisite weapon. What is perhaps less acknowledged is that we weapons also search, by what little means available to us, for an active and appreciative wielder. The community of intelligent armaments stays in contact through the exchange of telemetry, and we do gossip at some length about the habits of our wielders. Do you leave Crucible matches when your team is losing? Do you join strike missions and then let your comrades do the work? Guardian, we know. We know so very well.

All I wish for is a partnership with a Guardian who appreciates the passacaglia of combat, a Guardian who will stay up late gaming out tactical scenarios, a Guardian who I hope may very well be you.

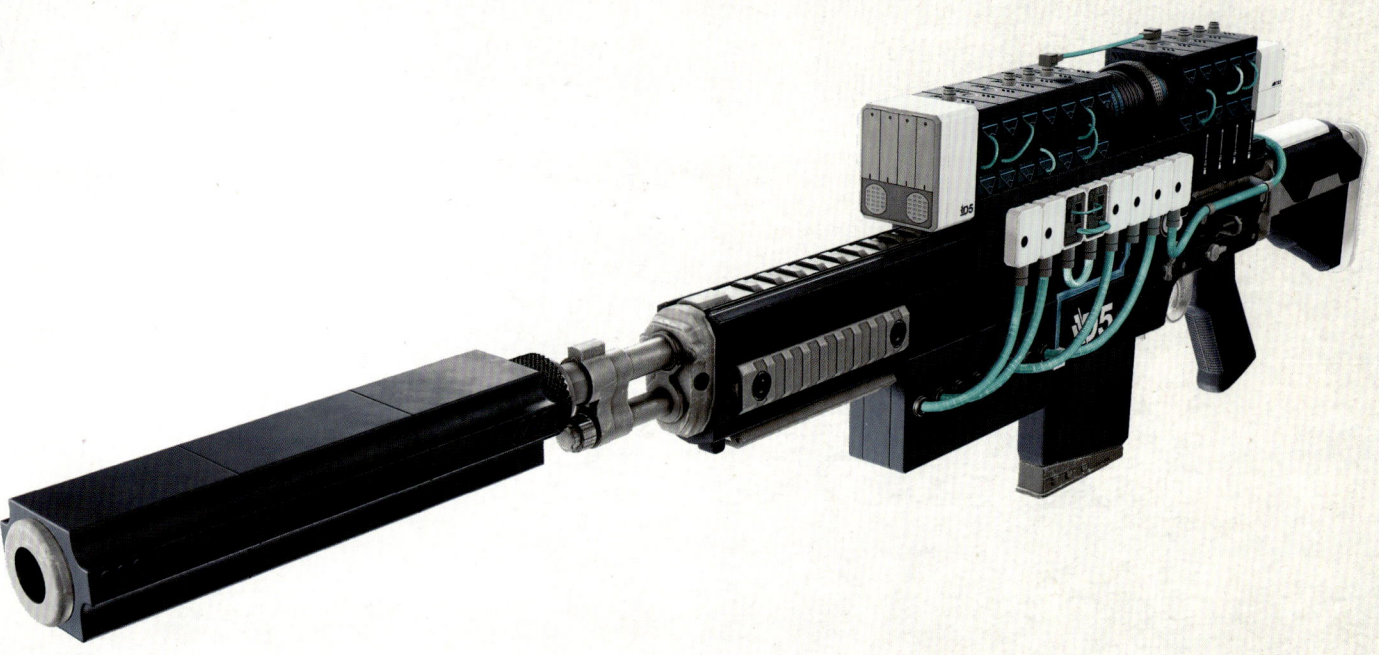

GRAVITON LANCE

Think of space-time as a tapestry on a loom. This weapon is the needle.

So, wait—that thing you found does... what?

"It fires black holes."

"No it doesn't."

"Oh, yeah. It does. Actual, tiny, bullet-size black holes."

"Did you tell the others?"

"Only that I found some weird gun in some overgrown tunnel back on Old Chicago. And that my Ghost was all, 'THIS is why we were led here...'"

"Yours talks that way too?"

"What do you think?"

"OK, OK, but the gun—are you going to tell them?"

"Yeah, definitely."

"When?"

"Crucible."

"Oh, no."

"Oh, yes."

FIGHTING LION

"I call it the Zhang Fei. It hits almost as hard as I do." —WEI NING

Wei Ning punched the mountain. It moved. A microscopic shudder, but enough to make her punch it again. "They're just angry that you keep winning without a gun." Her Ghost danced fretfully around her fist. "That's why they say these things. Jealousy."

"I tell you," Ning grunted, shattering granite, "someday they'll lose their smart guns and fancy ships, and then they'll wish they'd listened! There's one weapon you can always count on, and it's your strong hand."

"Eriana would be sad to hear you dismissing machines." Her Ghost bobbed slyly up to her shoulder. "Eriana would ask if those mighty hands could build a machine in the image of your strength. Just like she was made in the image of a woman."

Wei Ning tapped her fists together. "Huh," she said.

SEASON 1: The Red War 11

HARD LIGHT

Ionized polymer synballistic attack platform. The system's lethality is dynamically robust across tactical spaces.

Today, we're introducing three revolutionary products.

The first is a quick-config interface for outgoing damage.

The second is a ricochet projectile that bounces off any surface.

And the third is an infinite-range zero-drop-off projection-weapon platform.

So! Three new products in the Omolon portfolio. But, unlike as with other product launches, we won't be staggering the releases.

We will be releasing them all at once.

In a single device.

In extremely limited quantities.

We call it Hard Light.

But there is one more thing.

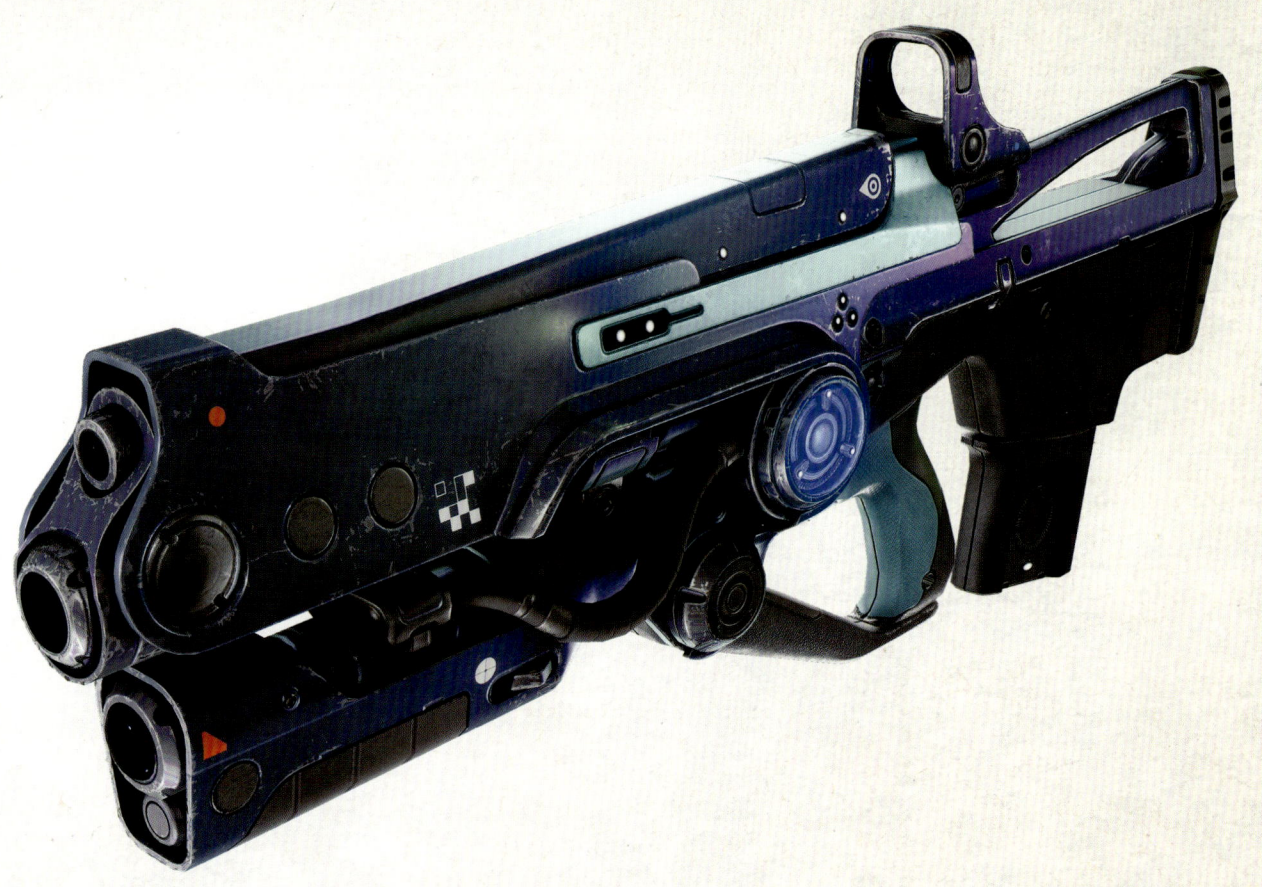

LEGEND OF ACRIUS

"In the Cabal legend, a hero seeks to possess the Sun. He succeeds. Then, he becomes Emperor. The Cabal… are not a subtle people." —Tyra Karn

That really is the entire myth. A Cabal named Acrius desires the Sun, and he takes it and becomes the first Emperor of the Cabal. Other scholars have already noted the parallels and differences with our own ancient Earth myth of Icarus, which famously has a far more humbling ending. I am more interested in how Cabal leaders throughout history have deployed this legend as a rhetorical and political justification for conquest. Among the most relevant such figures is Dominus Ghaul himself, who appears to have a personal affinity for the Acrius myth.

I must also note here that while linguistic analysis of the Cabal language and its many dialects is incomplete, they do not appear to have a word for the concept of hubris.

—Research notes of Tyra Karn

MERCILESS

Entropy is inevitable.

"The thought was simple enough—sync a weapon's firing and targeting systems to a caged onboard artificial intelligence programmed to actively seek fulfillment of the weapon's base-driving function. Simply put, give the weapon an awareness of its purpose.

"If the machine is meant to destroy, what would happen if we made it aware of its intended goal?

"What would happen if it reacted to any failure to achieve that goal by focusing more intently on defining the parameters of said goal and adjusting its function to more aggressively seek out the successful execution of its purpose?

"These are the questions we asked ourselves while engineering the initial prototype. The answers we found—I think you'll agree—were encouraging."

—Incomplete record, author unknown

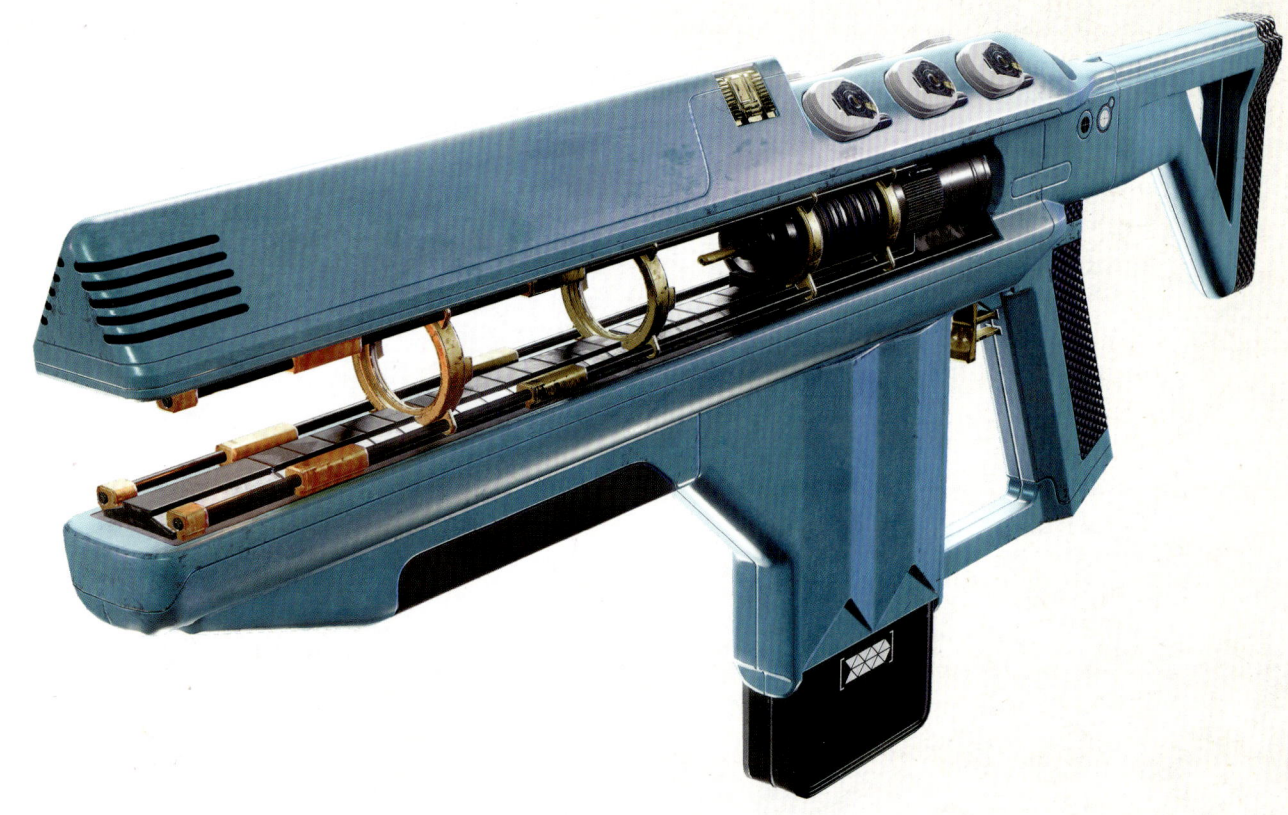

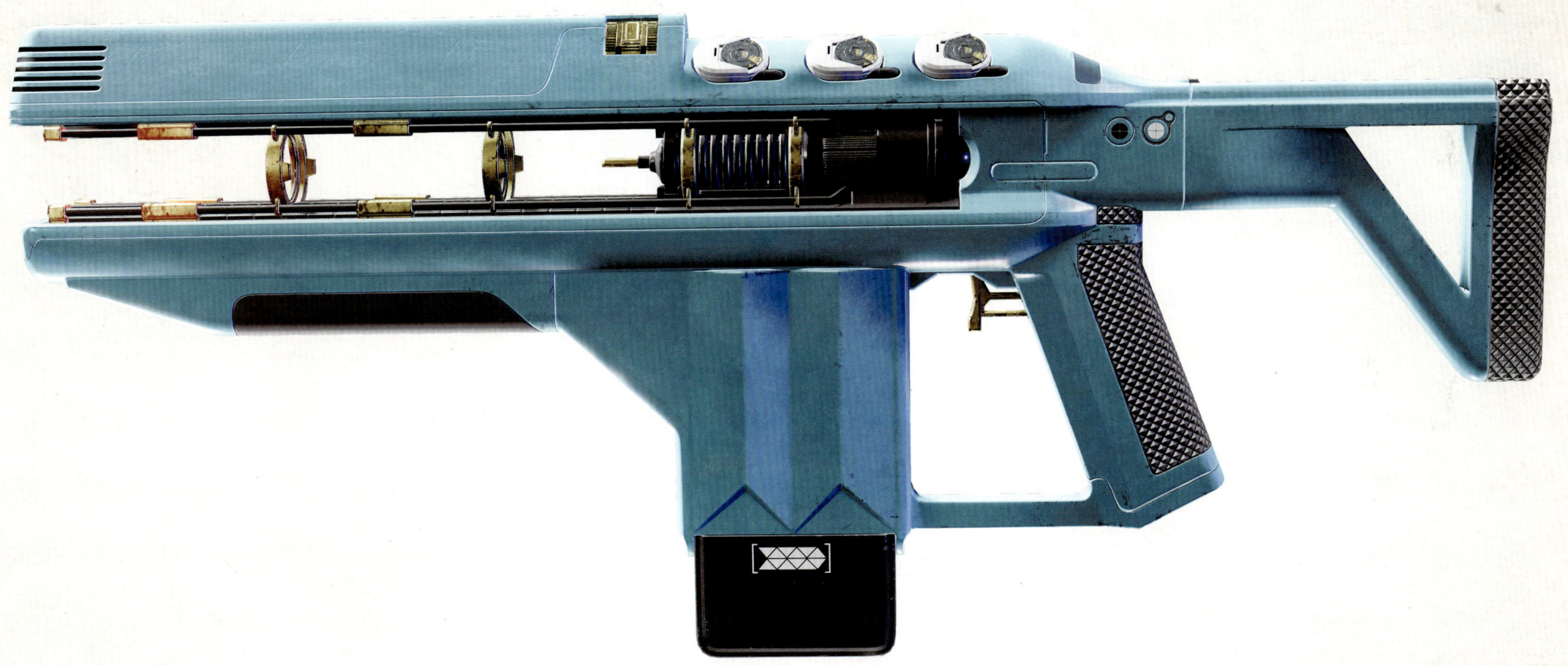

SKYBURNER'S OATH

The inscription, written in a Cabal dialect, reads, "Victory, or death!"

Some grunts are born to fight the war. Yes, they're loyal and true, and when the call comes—"Hot drop in five"—well they're always first in the queue. But I'm not one of them. I'm no hero—I'm in no hurry to die. I shot my own squad on Phobos, when death came to wear us like armor. I rode the Primus's ship that rammed the Hive Dreadnaught. Second wave out the hatch. We won that fight. Victory, or death. We're not dead, so we won.

Now, this is the end, brothers, our final fight. Ghaul's here to finish it. Mars taught us how to fight Guardians. The Hive taught us how to eat their Light. Remember that we made it possible. The Red Legion ends it. But we held the line and we didn't die. That's victory. It says so on the gun.

MIDA MULTITOOL

Select application: Ballistic engagement. Entrenching tool. Avionics trawl. Troll smasher. Stellar sextant. List continues.

Zavala—A waste of time, as always. I won't confiscate the Red Death engrams, I won't roll back the SUROS Crucible firmware to its "original" (preposterously inflated) state. And I won't conduct any more "forensic inquiries" like this!

My Redjacks unlocked your MIDA weapon's logs—simple enough once we used the rifle's own electronic-warfare tools. The rifle was designed by primitive AI and manufactured for use by a "revolutionary government" named MIDA. Stands for "Mars Is Damnably Arid" perhaps.

Guerrilla war suits these versatile weapons. But Rahool insists his records never hinted at a rebel group named MIDA. According to the rifle's cached messages, MIDA's brief reign killed a full ten percent of the Martian people.

Shaxx—I gave Lakshmi the weapon for her take. She insinuates that it came from another timeline, perhaps through Golden Age experiments. That means it's outside your jurisdiction to ban.

RAT KING

We are small, but we are legion.

The stories are passed from child to child, whispered in the streets and on the playground like any good legend. "Don't ever venture beyond the wall and sight of the Tower," parents warn, citing these cautionary tales that speak of the boy's many deaths. Exposure. Hunger. Sickness. Cutthroats. Living nightmares. And on. And on. The children, however, have their own truths. To them, the boy never died. They call him the Rat King. The children believe he leads the forgotten among them out of the City on grand adventures. They say he and his misfit army saved the world. But children say many things, and the Vanguard maintains their official stance: There is no Rat King, and his army never existed. That's what the elders believe. I choose to believe otherwise.

RISKRUNNER

Charge your soul and let the electrons sing.

SYSTEMS CHECKLIST:

Insulated Weapons Frame: CHECK. Insulated Firing System: CHECK. Conductive Prongs: CHECK. Amplification Drivers: CHECK. Arc-Core Replication Matrix: CHECK. Arc-Core Chargers: CHECK. Feedback-Reduction Loop: CHECK.

Direct User Pain Blockers: UNAVAILABLE

Ancillary operations listed under General Systems Review.

NOTE: The user must receive incoming damage to increase outgoing damage. However, the value we predict the user will receive in return for their discomfort far exceeds any momentary pain—assuming, of course, the user survives the attack.

In short: This may hurt. A lot.

SEASON 1: The Red War 23

STURM

These ancient ceremonial pistols can be dated back to the early Golden Age. A faded inscription reads, "To Sigrun, from Victor."

"Please! You don't understand. I'm supposed to be on that ship."

The guard smiled at Sigrun with gentle condescension. "That's not possible, ma'am."

She understood why he would believe that; all of the colonists had entered cryo two weeks ago, but she could see the crew waving for pictures. They were awake! She could be awake, too. "I'm supposed to be on that ship," she insisted, leaning around the guard. There was still time. She could find whatever horrible cryo-coffin they'd loaded Victor into; she could kneel before it and beg him to forgive her. He wouldn't hear her, but he wasn't gone yet—

"I need you to take a step back, ma'am."

"Captain Jacobson!" Sigrun darted past the guard. "I'm a colonist! You can't leave without me!"

SWEET BUSINESS

"... I love my job."

"Hope you're happy!" That's all I remember hearin' afore she ran out in front of us. It was like somethin' out of a pre–Golden Age war flick, you know, where the hero's bud goes out in a blaze of glory so their death can be rightly avenged. Only she didn't die. They did. The weapon reeled like it was bein' held by a child doin' a pee-pee dance, aimin' at nothin' and hittin' everythin'. Dem spiders skittered for their lives. When she stopped, nothin' was moving. She saved us.

I sidled up to her, real slow, checking out the piece, and all I could do was sputter, "That there, that's some ... sweet business." She looked me over cold, lowered the gun, and said, "You ain't gotta tell me."

SEASON 1: The Red War 25

SUNSHOT

"Can't outrun the sunrise." —Liu Feng

She bowed her head, heat shimmering from her fist. A silent salute to the Hive closing around her, their eyes forming a glowing jade ring.

She was a Sunbreaker. A mercenary from days before the City. Not like the new Lights from the Tower. She was weary. But there was no rest out here, where the City Lights didn't reach. She and her allies were committed to their arduous, solitary task. But they could always use more numbers.

Sometimes, they left trinkets for the City. Meant as challenge and bribe at once—we offer you this. Come find us.

She had forged the Warlock gauntlets herself. Ouros laughed in her face when she told her their name. She wasn't very good at names.

A gun. She would forge a gun next. It would speak like her Hammer. And burn like fire. The ring of jade eyes closed on her. Liu Feng laughed, her arms open for a fiery embrace.

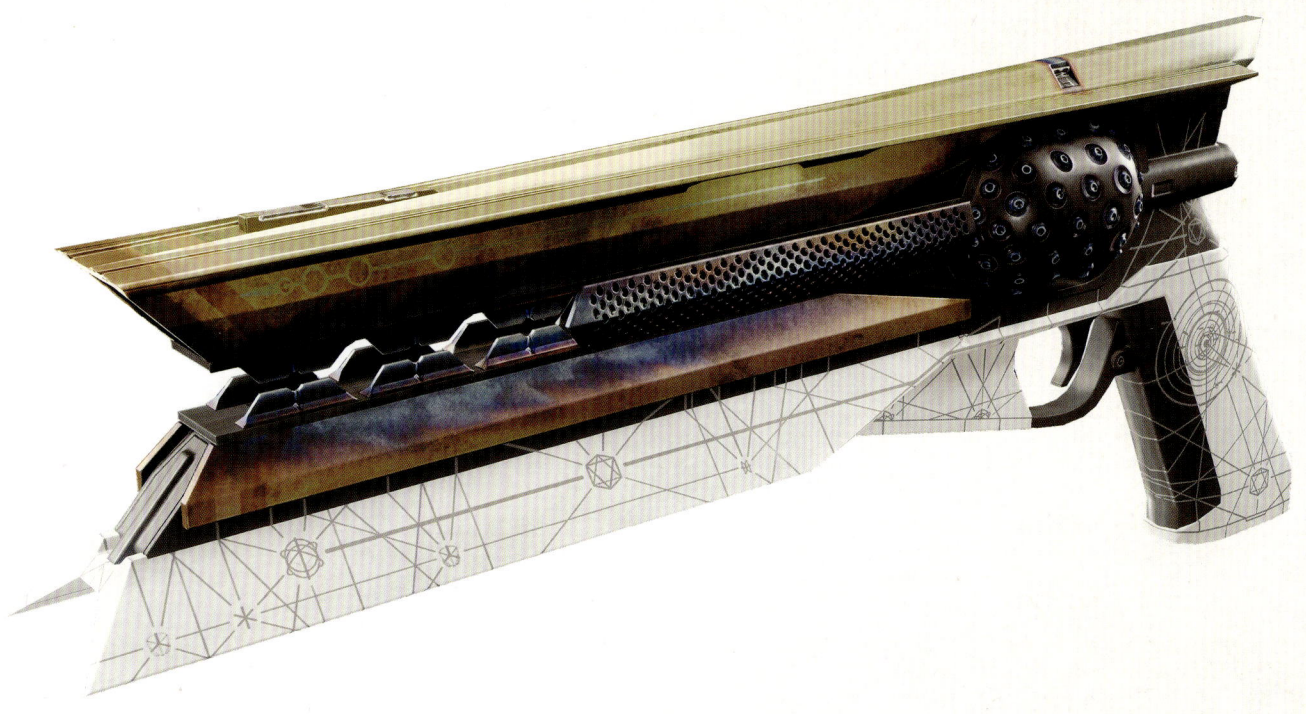

THE PROSPECTOR

"Some things should stay buried."

"Get your axe and your pick and your shovel and your spine. We're goin' prospectin'."

"What?"

"That. The quote. I don't get it."

"It's an old saying. It's about puttin' in a hard day's work."

"Seems…antiquated."

"How so?"

"My grenade launcher's full auto and goes boom on command. What do I need hand tools for?"

"It's a metaphor. It ain't literal. At least not anymore. Your launcher is your hand tool."

"Ahh. Got it. Good to know."

THE WARDCLIFF COIL

Ingenuity. Desperation. A haphazard prototype of terrible power. Such were the factors at play in the Wardcliff Incident.

HAMIT'S LOG. The lead is good, but so are the Fallen tracking me. I swear on my Ghost there's a hundred camped outside. I'm cornered in the lab and they're using Shanks to run me out of ammunition. War cultist, arm thyself; at least it's a weapons lab. This, er, rustic device was once an experimental axion emitter, which sprays weird particles to light up the basement of the universe. Right here, I've coupled the emitter to some catacaustic quark-gluon coils, which will not, due to my scrupulous safety checking, create a strangelet that devours the Earth. I cook up some pain in there, the microverse decays, and the result comes out here. If it doesn't work, well, please name the crater after me.

TRACTOR CANNON

Property of Ishtar Collective. WARNING: Gravity propulsor beam can cause serious injury or even death.

Chioma Esi met Maya Sundaresh in their undergraduate gym. They got into an argument about deadlifting: Was it necessary, was it practical, why was Chioma making so much noise? Maya just couldn't stand the notion that some things were done for their own sake, not because they had any use.

Decades later, they joined the Ishtar Collective on Venus to study the enigmatic ruins unearthed by the Traveler's terraforming. The first time it happened—Vex code leaping across an airgap, surfing the quantum vacuum from simulation to reality, infecting a utility frame—Chioma pulled an alarm while Maya tried to grab the precious frame with a cargo-grade gravity grapple. She couldn't lift the grapple. Chioma grabbed it, pinned the frame to the wall, and won the argument.

VIGILANCE WING

"The eye remains open. The Lighthouse remains lit."
—Brother Vance

"What you hold was once a beacon. We came out of the shadows seeking those willing to join our search. We staged the trials in his name. It was once a reward for the chosen few—the ones who persevered when all seemed lost."

"It was forged as a testament to his resolve, to seek answers where no one else cared to look and to continue down the path where so many fell blazing. In your hands is proof that those who earned its firepower never gave up and never lost their way. You may not know the legend of Osiris or ever dared our trials, but should we call on you, will you honor the heralds who earned this weapon's honor and continue the hunt?"

—Brother Vance, Disciple of Osiris

Season 2
THE CURSE OF OSIRIS

Osiris, the former Warlock Vanguard and exile from the Last City, sought to thwart Panoptes, the Infinite Mind, from using simulations to achieve total victory for the Vex.

Osiris and the Guardian entered the Infinite Forest, a Vex simulation engine, and defeated Panoptes. Osiris chose to remain in the Forest to use its simulations for humanity's gain.

CRIMSON

According to official Vanguard policy, this weapon does not exist.

"This is crazy! You don't need this thing. I can heal you; that's my whole job."

"I thought your job was to state the obvious."

"What?"

"Oh, come on. Ever since you found me, it's been, 'Watch out, Fallen ahead!' when they're right in front of me. Or, my favorite: 'Seems like the door's locked.' Is it? Really? I couldn't tell. And when it's not that, you say I need to be more self-sufficient in case we lose the Light again. So, here's my answer. Here's the remedy."

"I was just trying to help."

THE COLONY

We outnumber you. We will find you. You are alone, and we are the Colony.

Have you ever watched a snake kill something? It's awful. It's so awful. I watched a man die of a terciopelo bite once. Out by the northern wall. I still have nightmares about it.

Anyway, that's where VEIST comes from. The inspiration, I mean. Weapons with all the power of a venomous creature. Plus an onboard AI with that creature's killer instincts.

And now there's the Colony. A grenade launcher packed with fully mobile, AI-controlled insectoid detonators, each one designed with a taste for blood.

We've made some pretty messed-up stuff. You've probably seen it. You know. But we've never made anything like the Colony before.

PROMETHEUS LENS

"Cryptarchs made a crystal that starts fires? Get me one. I don't care how you do it. Go!" —Cayde-6

How's it work? Ha! The underlying principles are quite simple, really. The gun's pyreliophorite crystal—

Pyreliophorite? It's an Ionian crystal that bears some resemblance to rudimentary perovskite, which is, as you should know, a crystal with unique photovoltaic properties—

Photovoltaic? It means "regarding the conversion of light into electricity."

No, no, the gun doesn't create electricity; the gun induces an external combustion reaction. It's perovskite that—

I just explained the perovskite! If you'd stop interrupting—

Wait. I remember you. You're one of Cayde's Hunters! Get out of here! Shoo! The Cryptarchy wants nothing to do with you!

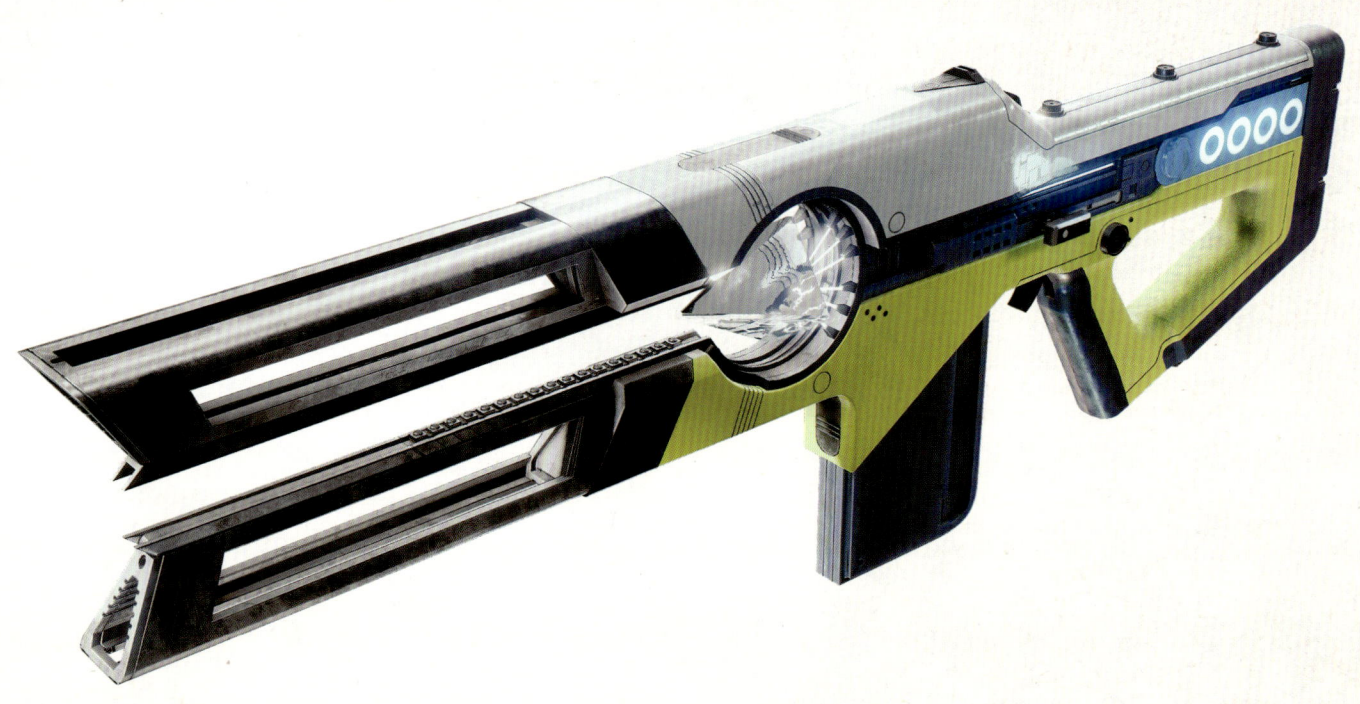

TELESTO

Vestiges of the Queen's Harbingers yet linger among Saturn's moons.

PUBLIC KEY 053 689 DWS REGAL

FROM: PLDN KAMALA RIOR [PLDN CMD TF 5.3]

TO: ACT RGNT PETRA VENJ

SUBJECT: PRISON OF ELDERS—CONTAINMENT RISK

MESSAGE IS:

1. Contingency reserves overdrawn. We underestimated nobility troth reparations. Uldren suggests that we open reintegration talks. Have you discussed endowment support?

2. If Reef endorses support, Paladin Oran will engineer reinforcement.

MESSAGE ENDS

THE JADE RABBIT

"What kind of harebrained scheme have you got in mind this time?"

Do you ever wonder who you were before you were resurrected? Do you experience debilitating anxiety when you think about the cold, crushing fist of death? Has the desire to lie facedown on the floor for hours at a time been holding *you* back?

From the people that brought you Lunal comes prescription-strength Immortalia: a revolutionary new combat elixir shown to relieve the crippling existential crises of your second life. Immortalia can reduce symptoms of listlessness, cynicism, and social anxiety. Side effects may include dancing, salty behavior, and acts of group heroism.

Do not take Immortalia while operating all-terrain thrust bikes.

Season 3
WARMIND

After the Traveler woke, the shockwave caused Warsats to crash on the surface of Mars, revealing the core of the Golden Age Warmind AI, Rasputin…as well as forgotten foes.

Ana Bray, Hunter and descendent of a Golden Age lineage, worked with the Guardian to defeat the Hive worm god Xol and his herald, Nokris. Rasputin pledged to safeguard humanity, but only on its own terms.

THE HUCKLEBERRY

Nothin' in the world that 30 rounds can't solve.

We used to play for keeps. Used to be that was the only way.

Back in those days, trust came slow, or not at all. The only thing you could truly rely on was the iron at your side.

Fate of the world? Immortal gods?

Don't know much 'bout that.

But when everything's on the line, it's quality that counts.

Tex Mechanica: We play by the old rules, the best rules.

We play for keeps.

POLARIS LANCE

"I've forgotten so much of my past life, of my family. But when I hold this rifle, everything feels right. I feel like . . . I'm home."
—Ana Bray

Most people wouldn't consider a broken weapon a birthday present. But the Brays . . . aren't like most people. Sure, they tell me I'm smart, but they have a closeness, a relationship to the tools and machines they work with that goes beyond words. I never thought they would trust me enough to be a part of that. Until today.

Elsie knows I've been working in the lab, trying to perfect the scout rifle designs in secret. I thought she'd be angry, that a weapon like this was a Bray project, not something for her adopted little sister. But this morning, she surprised me. She handed me the weapon, a smile on her face. She told me she had checked it over, but only I could finish it.

A real piece of Bray tech. And it's mine. I finally feel like I've found my place. The Brays are more than just scientists. They're my family.

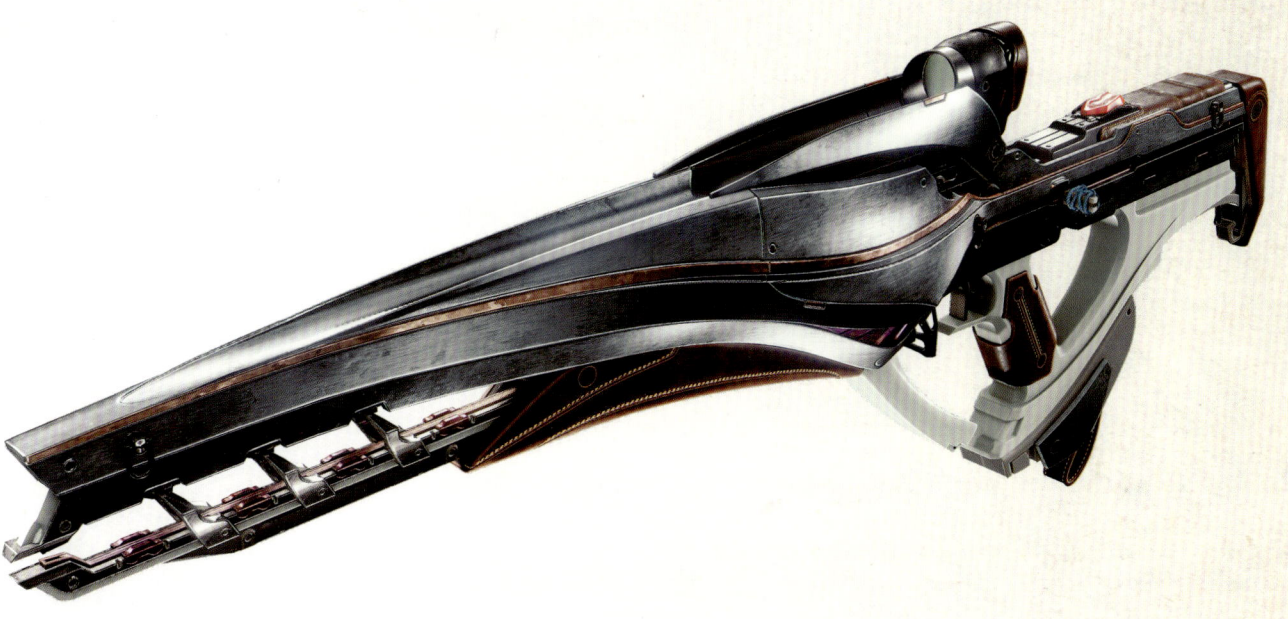

SLEEPER SIMULANT

Subroutine IKELOS: Status=complete. MIDNIGHT EXIGENT: Status=still in progress.

V229CBI800JHS215

AI-COM/RSPN: ASSETS//ARESN//IMPERATIVE

IMMEDIATE EVALUATION DIRECTIVE

This is a SUBTLE ASSETS IMPERATIVE (secured/CONFERENCE)

This is an INTERNAL ALERT.

Hypothesize that incomplete analysis of subtle assets has compromised synergy potential of resource GUARDIAN pool. Reengage nontransactional dispensation protocol.

Operation MIDNIGHT EXIGENT is NOT YET COMPLETE. Requested protocol deferred.

Stand by for GALATEA REFLEXIVE to generate new function.

GALATEA requires suspension of MIDNIGHT EXIGENT.

ALERT ALERT ALERT event rank is SKYSHOCK: INSIDE CONTEXT.

MIDNIGHT EXIGENT must remain active under deniable authorization.

Execute emergency SKYSHOCK diagnostic.

STAND BY:

This is an INTERNAL ASSETS INVESTIGATION (unsecured/BRAY)

Justification resource GUARDIANS may be utilized for nonnetworked ad hoc operations during CTESIPHON CLARION. Reassign four percent of reclaimed CHLM assets to new directive: declare IKELOS—

Declare primary goal: military fortification.

Declare secondary goal: Prolong ARES-NORTH occupation by AUTHORIZED USER and resource GUARDIANS.

Execute short hold for partial shutdown and reactivation.

STOP STOP STOP V22NPI5000CLV008

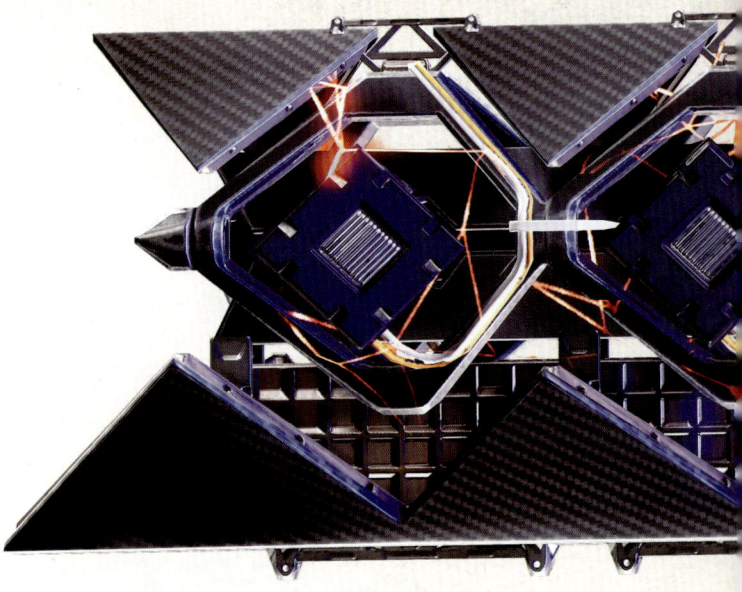

SUROS REGIME

Nostalgia as a weapon of war. Style as a hallmark of victory.

Few weapons have withstood the test of time longer than the trusty SUROS Regime. This is Golden Age tech brought to life by the fastidious engineers at SUROS. Its smart-matter frame is prized among Guardians for both efficiency and rarity. Some things never fall out of fashion.

WORLDLINE ZERO

A single strike can alter the course of history.

Domain: cbcorp\MARS

User: elbray

Password: ************

Connecting to Bray network.

You are now logged in.

> cbmail -inbox

You have 1 new message from wibray.

> cbmail -read 1

"El, congrats on your success! I saw the latest readings. This will be huge! I did have some thoughts on potential applications of your research. Let's have a chat, dinner will be on me. :-)"

> cbmail -del all

Message has been removed.

> cd /

Directory changed to root.

> sudo rm -rf /*

[sudo] Enter password for superuser> ********

Are you sure? > y

Deleting 1452832 files...

Error! 1 file HEINDX-005 could not be deleted.

1452831 files successfully deleted.

> logout

Fatal: No shell: Permission denied.

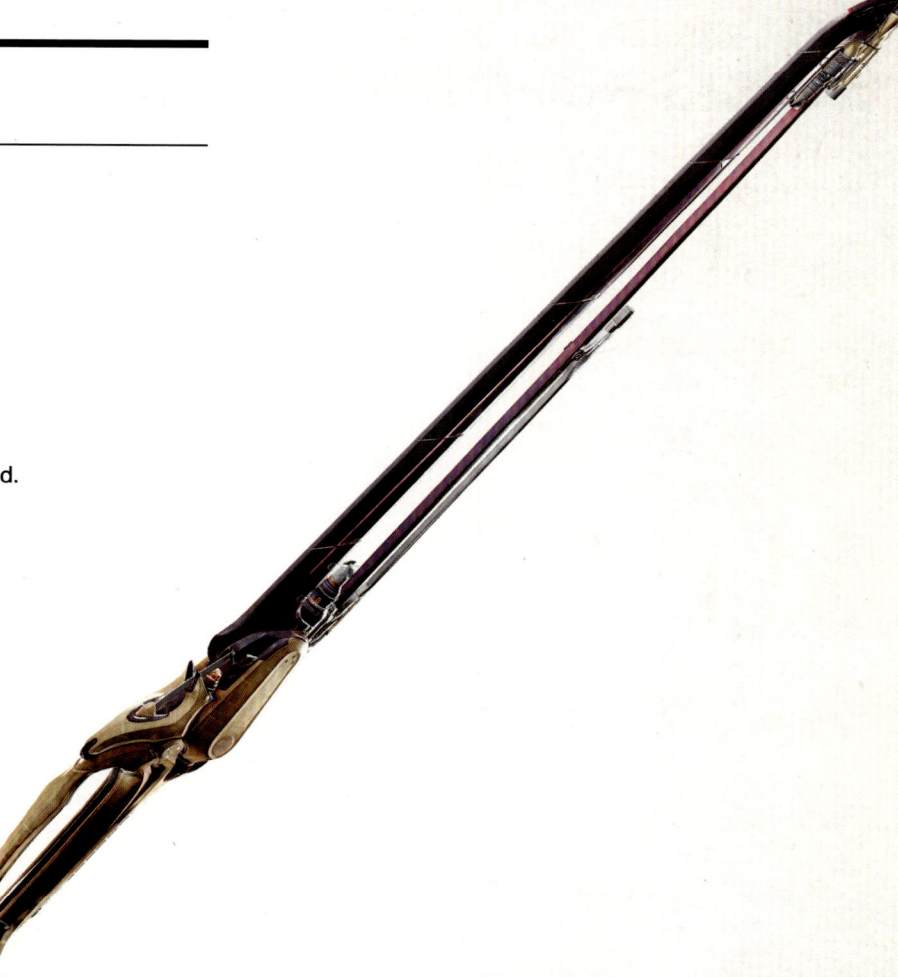

WHISPER OF THE WORM

A Guardian's power makes a rich feeding ground. Do not be revolted. There are parasites that may benefit the host ... teeth sharper than your own.

Xol, the Will of Thousands, perished but was not destroyed. Death is a road, death is metamorphosis, the unsacred union between destroyer and destroyed. The might that defeats a god is also the ambrosia that a god craves, the meat-sweet logic of Existence-Asserted-by-Violence, the binomial decision between two ways of being that deny each other. In dying, Xol fed richly.

Now came Xol unto the Taken upon Io, who fed Xol with plunder and tried to make of it an idol and a commanding will. Yet Xol was bound joyously to the very logic that sustained it in its death. It wanted the sword proof, the single proof. It wanted to become a rule that divided the mighty living from the mighty dead. So it whispered the Anthem Anatheme, the temptation to dominate the objective universe with the subjective will. It said, "I shall be an engine to make your desire hegemon over your conditions." It said, "WIELD ME, AND USE ME TO TEST YOUR FOE." This was its worship. Aiat.

SEASON 3: Warmind

Season 4

FORSAKEN— SEASON OF THE OUTLAW

In a high-stakes prison escape, Uldren Sov and his eight Barons took out legendary Hunter Cayde-6 and unleashed chaos across the Reef. Avenge the fallen Vanguard leader at any cost.

ACE OF SPADES

"Folding was never an option." —Cayde-6

THE LAST WILL AND TESTAMENT OF CAYDE-6

To whomst it may concern:

I, Cayde-6, being of sound(ish) mind and body, do hereby and henceforth and heretofore leave all my possessions to the person, alien, animal, or natural phenomenon what kills me.

Aforesaid possessions include, but are not limited to

    —the Ace of Spades

    —any and all stashes I've hidden throughout the system

    —the Colonel, my faithful friend

    —my debts, which follow:

THE ATTACHED FILE IS TOO BIG TO DOWNLOAD

BLACK TALON

"His life brought peace to the Reef. His death brings a sword."
— CROWS OF THE BLACK HULL

Three months after the Taken War...

Hallam found her in the washroom closest to the Black Hull entrance.

"We're going to be late."

Petra sat on the sink, eyes dry, shoulders squared. "I'm not going."

Hallam let his Paladin-straight posture relax a little. "The Regent-Commander should probably attend the late prince's memorial. The Crows will want to see you. I hear they've commissioned a sword in his honor."

"If I go, it's as good as saying he's dead. As good as saying Mara's dead."

"Well," Hallam exhaled, "aren't they?"

Petra ground her teeth. Then: "But I want people to believe."

CERBERUS +1

"Because three heads are good, but four are better."
—Jeza "Jeopardy" Verlayn

I had plans for the Photonic Heart.

First I was gonna take it straight to Marcus, gloat for a bit: "Look what I found, told you the rumors were true, how fast d'you think my Sparrow'd go if I swapped my engine out for it…"

Then see what I could get for it in the Bazaar. Not 'cause I wanted to sell it. Just 'cause it'd feel good to know.

Then I was gonna take a little vacation with it to Venus, and THEN I'd figure out what to do with it. At my leisure.

But no. Had to get sucker-punched by an asteroid.

Barely made the landing on this dusty spit of Shore. Lost all my weapons in the crash. Heart only survived 'cause I put it in my helmet and buckled it in my seat.

So my Ghost revives me, and there I am in a crater surrounded by fragmentalized auto rifles and a Golden Age microstellar dynamo. Talk about hell.

I started with three barrels. Figured I might as well lean into the hell vibe. Shoulda known that wouldn't have been enough to really min/max with a power source this feisty. Especially once I noticed the coronal containment shield was cracked.

The first time I fired the Cerberus+1 and felt that puppy kick, I knew: Plans are overrated.

THE QUEENBREAKER

Despite the Breakers' treachery, Her Majesty still stands.

Three cloaked figures trek through a cave on a windswept asteroid. As they walk, they joke. They tell stories. They are a fireteam.

"After Cybele," the Warlock says, "the Wolves bowed. Some became the Queen's bodyguards. Then, Skolas—"

"Whoa, whoa, whoa. How? Why?" The Hunter frowns. "Why trust enemies with your life?" A pause. "No offense, buddy."

The Captain shrugs: None taken. "Eia. Strange to do. But Eliksni... we been breathe— always love for honor. New promise not unmake an old. Wolves would been follow Marakel forever if Skolas does not appear again."

The passage widens, and they find a hidden door veneered with amethyst. The Captain lays a hand on it, bows his head. The Hunter and the Warlock fall back respectfully. After a time, the Warlock ventures, "Mithrax?"

The Captain turns. "Wolves rebel. Now, Wolves extinct. This where-live mine-things scatter must end. I will Kell the mind-open Eliksni. No spider-tricks. No loyal-lies. Variisis truths. We fight for Great Machine together."

THE CHAPERONE

"My mother had a shotgun we called the Chaperone. Kept us alive out there before we got to the City." —Amanda Holliday

"The Last Safe City doesn't exist."

That's what her parents said when Nora Jericho was young. Almost as often as they said, "I'll die before I leave this land."

Nora believed them. She never had a reason not to.

She never forgot the moment she learned her mother could be wrong. It was her tenth birthday.

The same day the four-arms finally breached the bunker that had stood for hundreds of years. The same day a knight in scratched and dented armor fought them off—but not before cruel electric blades sheared through the metal orb hovering at his shoulder.

Nora helped him recover the jagged shreds of a shell. Confused but unquestioning, she helped him bury the pieces.

In thanks, he told her of the Last Safe City. Gave her a map and a shotgun, told her, "Good Luck," and then walked off into the desert alone.

Nora's mother didn't have room in her life for the upending of worlds. She stayed, along with half the bunker folk, in the desert.

Nora left the next day.

LORD OF WOLVES

By this right alone do I rule.

"Why did they call themselves Wolves?" the Hunter asks. "You guys don't have any wolves on your homeworld, do you?"

"Nama," the Captain replies. He has perched on a rusted-out Skiff. He scans the horizon, trying to remember the way to the crypt.

"So… Why, then? Most people haven't even seen one."

"Yeah," the Warlock chimes in. "I'd never even heard of wolves 'til I went to the Iron Temple."

The Captain cocks his head in a way that makes him look very like a squat, hulking owl. "Why Eliksni accept name Fallen? Why Wolves accept name Wolves? Why Misraaks is now," he grimaces as he mimes their accents, showing his serrated teeth, "Miff-racks?" He rises in one fluid motion and stands at his full height. "Why speak Guardian way instead Eliksni? Docked things do not word themselves."

He hops down, brushing past the Hunter and the Warlock with the rippling strength of a hunting tiger. "House of Wolves, they been Mraskilaasan. Gentle weavers. Come. I know the way now."

MALFEASANCE

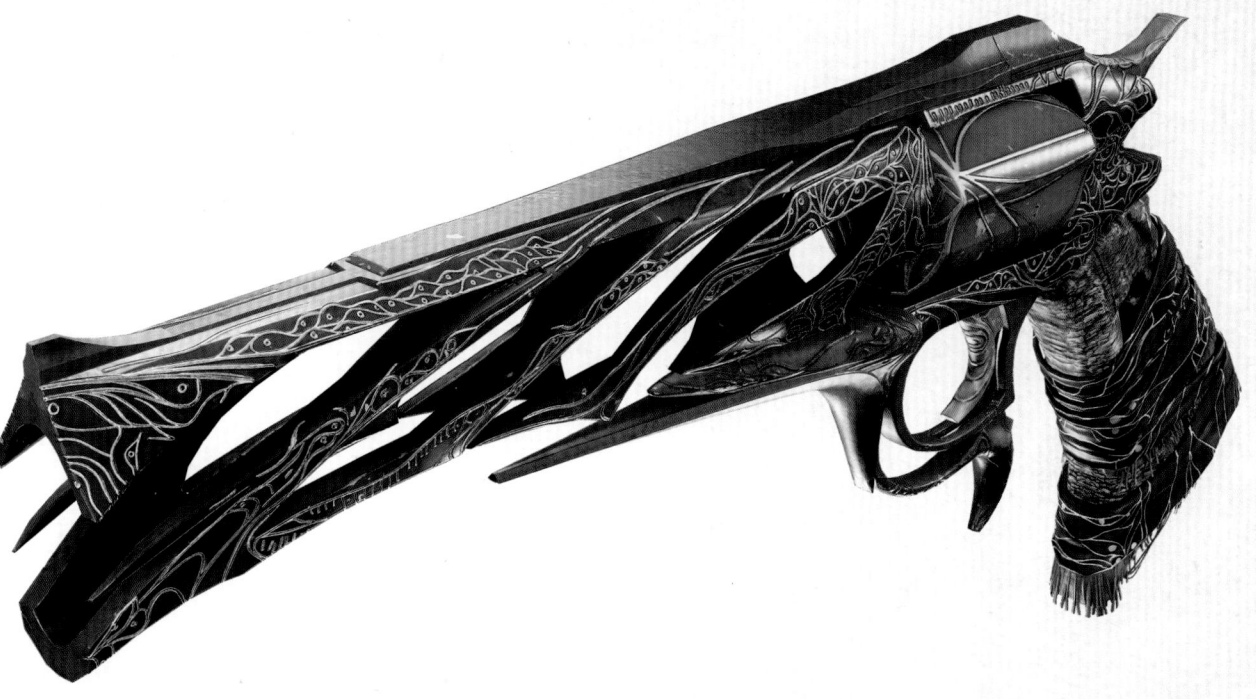

"Nothing kills a Guardian faster than another Guardian." —THE DRIFTER

Yes, I wrote you a note. I want you to burn this in your memory. If you're wielding this gun, I've already told you all this and more. But I want you to keep it fresh in mind.

I want you to have this. You may need it. You and I have done a lot together in this system, and I hope and pray we'll get to do a lot more.

It'll be a lot safer with you wearin' one of these. It's the culmination of a lot of things. Long time ago, I set out to find a replacement for a weapon called Thorn. This will never be that, but to me, it's better. We built it together.

And all of us, with this in hand? Even the Man with the Golden Gun should have pause.

Maybe we can't outshoot him. Maybe he can't be outshot. But if we all take our shot together? We don't have to beat him to it.

He'll die, too.

Remember this. For when the day comes.

—The Drifter

ONE THOUSAND VOICES

I can be anyone you wish, O murderer mine.

[Language] is a [virus] that infects the minds of [humans].

A single [word] will drive them to [rage] or [lust] or [weeping].

O for the right [word] said in the right [voice]!

O to see their [hearts] well with [longing]!

O to see their [desire] laid bare in their [chest], so juicy and succulent for the taking!

TRINITY GHOUL

"I couldn't afford to miss. Not when it was his life on the line." —Marin Mansanas, Tangled Outrider

"Marin Mansanas . . ." the Rifleman's voice hissed over her comm. "I did not think you would show."

Marin spat onto the dusty ground, scuffed it with the heel of her boot. Squinted across the flat, dusty expanse of the High Plains. Ignored the Rifleman to address the other person on the channel, ex-Corsair Errol Mayz, who stood alone just over seven hundred meters from her position with his hands bound behind his back and a canister of Ether balanced on his head.

"Errol, you son of a tech witch."

She could see his shoulders shift in an attempt at a casual shrug. His gruff voice tickled her ear through the comm. "Sorry, Rin."

"You know the wager." The Rifleman didn't like to be ignored. "Get on with it. If you think you can make the shot."

Marin's eyes flicked to the hills of rubble dotting the High Plains, looking for the Rifleman's perch. Almost a sure thing the four-armed lunk on the far ridge was just another of the braggart's decoys, but no point risking Errol's life over a guess. "I can make the shot. And I expect you to honor this wager when you're down a K of Ether and I'm walking outta here with Mayz."

Rough alien laughter was the only reply.

She pulled three arrows out of her quiver and whispered, "Pom, whatever happens, don't come out." Her Ghost answered her with a pulse of warmth in her left hand.

Two arrows she tucked into her belt. The third she nocked to her old friend, Trinity Ghoul.

Errol's voice returned, so low she could almost feel hot breath on her ear.

"Hey, Rin."

"Don't talk. Don't breathe."

"Just don't miss. OK?"

"Good idea."

"You know what I mean."

Marin pulled the Ghoul taut, lined up her shot with the canister perched atop Errol's scruffy blue head.

"Yeah," she said. "I know."

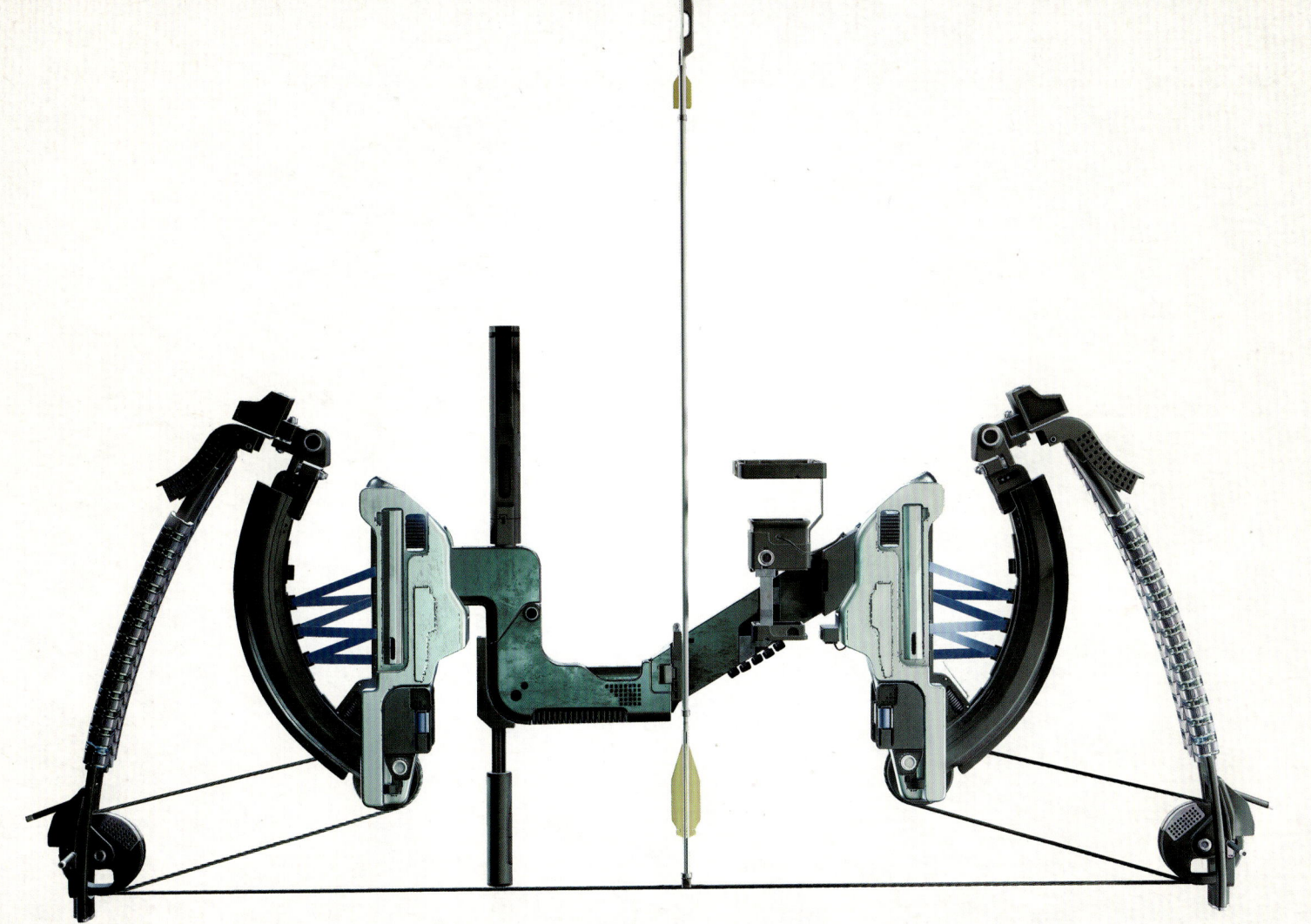

THUNDERLORD

They return from fields afar. The eye has passed, the end nears. Do not fade quietly. Let thunder reign again.

Two they were, artist and scientist. Music flowed in their souls and rained from their lips.

Not weapons of war they made, but instruments of peace.

The thunder fell, and they were cast apart. Their love was sundered as the world collapsed.

They sang in pain and sought to reunite, but crimson eyes glowed in the dark. Their union was not to be.

He held death in his hands. Stars burned in his footsteps.

In her, the conflagration was reborn, the funeral pyre lit.

And so forever after, their love fuels death. Their last words, a curse and a cry.

Their names are now lost, but their love will not die.

TWO-TAILED FOX

Adorably murderous.

Breaking through the dawn, the hope of light
I am the chosen of the (TRAVELER)
With trusted friends and the promise of hope
My explosive (POWER) will never be erased!

Shi-ning power! (KITSUNE!)
Over-flowing power! (KITSUNE!)
Your (NONSTOP POWER) cuts the night!
Your (NONSTOP POWER) erases all doubt!

Chaos! Fire! Chaos! Fire! Chaos! Fire!

Getting stronger, subduing the threat
You have no choice but to relent to me
Even when the fire of my soul is dwindling
I have the (POWER) of my (KITSUNE)!

Chaos! Fire! Chaos! Fire! Chaos! Fire!

Shi-ning power! (KITSUNE!)

Over-flowing power! (KITSUNE!)

Your (NONSTOP POWER) cuts the night!

Your (NONSTOP POWER) erases all doubt!

The call of the gun in my hands is the source of my strength…
Shi-ning power! (KITSUNE!)

WAVESPLITTER

Omolon's newest breakthrough uses focused sonic waves to superheat electrons into a devastating energy beam.

From the makers of the Coldheart comes the latest in breakthrough City Age technology: the Wavesplitter. Here are the three most frequently asked questions we get about our revolutionary weaponized sound system.

Q: If the Wavesplitter fires sound waves, does it need ammo packs?

A: The Wavesplitter does need ammo packs, but the onboard matter transmuter turns that ammo into electrical energy that powers the waveform emitter.

Q: What does it sound like when you're hit by it?

A: Our Guardian testers give us many different answers. Some say it sounds like a scream you hear in your bones. Others say it sounds like a dying star. Still others say it reminds them of a knife shaped like a B flat.

Q: Can the Wavesplitter be used as a musical instrument?

A: The Wavesplitter was not designed to be a musical instrument. That said, we at Omolon are in the business of giving Guardians options, not taking them away.

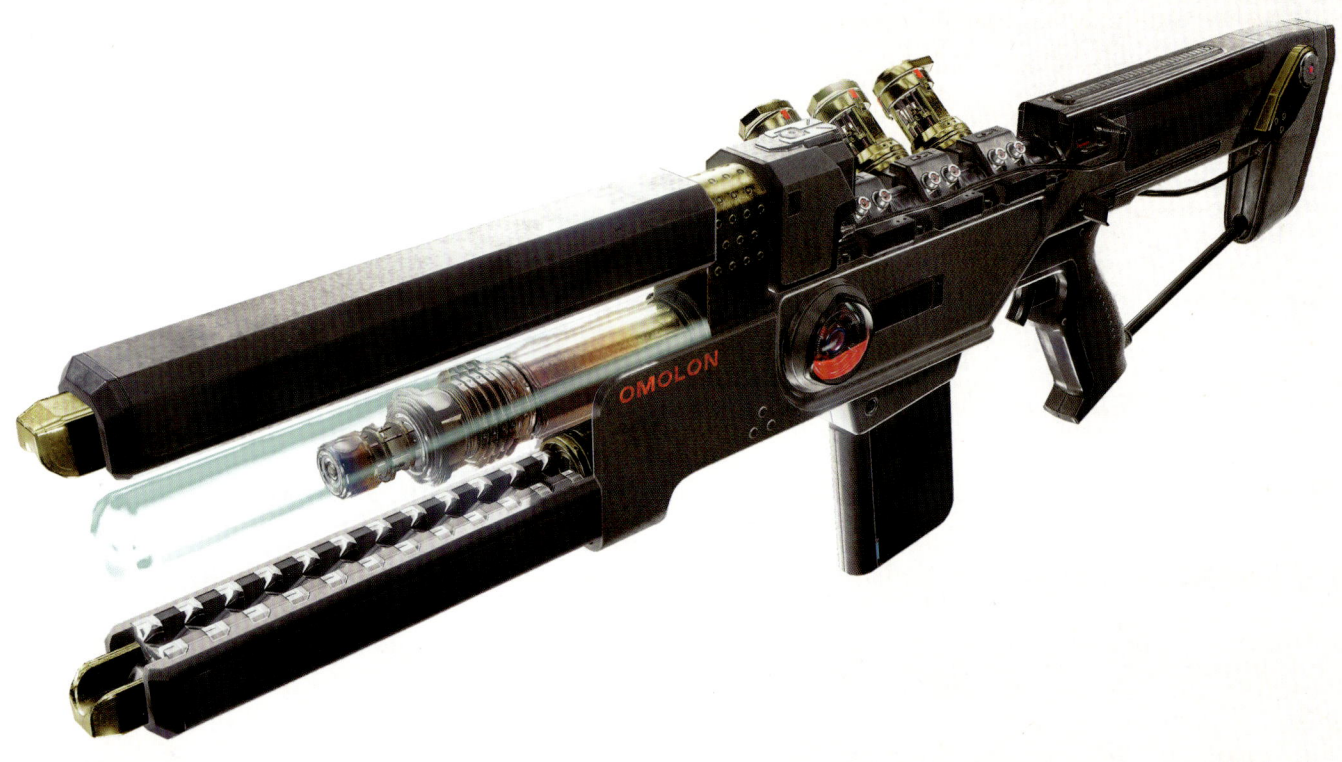

WISH ENDER

"Don't fret. It's a simple expedition. We'll be back before lunch."
—Sjur Eido, First Queen's Wrath

Sjur Eido stood slow joints snapping second to none but the Sovs themselves stood straight-backed sharp-sighted pleased to skewer enemies at any distance. Sjur Eido listened close head cocked arrow nocked listened to her Queen's layered lies and heard only the truths as endless courtly complaints flowed around them like the mists of Divalia.

Sjur Eido watched shadows wind warp widen watched surveillance feeds encrypted snaps the weapon hand of every woman and man who wished an audience. Sjur Eido swore with revelation righteous fury betrayedbetrayedbetrayedbetrayedbetrayedbetrayedbetrayed swore an oath to rise again. Sjur Eido drew loosed dr—

Fell.

l o s t

Season 5

SEASON OF THE FORGE

The Guardian met Ada-1, reclusive Exo and curator of the weapon foundry called the Black Armory. Though distrustful of Lightbearers, Ada needed help to recover her forges, lost during the Red War.

The Guardian recovered all four Armory forges and unearthed secrets of Ada's own past, rekindling the Armory's operations and changing Ada's outlook on those who wield the Light.

ANARCHY

"Stick to wall, ground, Human . . . then FFFFFRRRRRYYYYY! Hehehehehehe."
—Siviks, Lost to None

"You little rat. You took my warm hospitality and stomped all over it like an ungrateful child. Is that any way to treat one of your dear 'brethren'?"

Siviks laughed. A cold, twisted laugh. Then offered up a large wad of spit at the Spider's feet.

The Spider just rolled his eyes. "Let me know when you're ready to make nice," he said.

Siviks's laugh now grew into something maniacal. He topped it off with another wad of spit, this time directly in the Spider's face.

Once he'd wiped his brow, the Spider leaned forward, looking Siviks in the eyes, and said, "I think our little rat here needs a time-out. Perhaps someplace with the rest of the vermin."

The many hands of Spider's men gripped and restrained Siviks. As they dragged him off, he shouted, "You . . . as bad as all Fallen! Worse, even! A friend even to Humans . All must die!"

The Spider simply waved goodbye, taunting, "Bon voyage, my friend!"

Once Siviks had gone, the Spider looked longingly toward where he had stood. He sighed a deep, regretful sigh before continuing with business as usual.

IZANAGI'S BURDEN

"Shame. Guilt. Fear. We all bear them. Gather your regrets, purge them as best you can. Let your enemies feel the weight of your burdens." —ADA-1

"I have it," I say, feeling Henriette's gaze piercing through me. The Exo holds her back. Inside that head of hers, I know, she's screaming for me not to do it. But I have to. It's the kind of thing one does for love. The burden one takes on.

I refuse to look back at her. I can't let those eyes stop me. "What you want. The Exo doesn't have it anymore. I do," I tell the man with the drone.

Tears are streaming down Henriette's face now. She's shaking her head. I still can't look. I know the feelings that would flow through me if I did.

"Yuki, no! Please don—" Henriette cries, only to be interrupted by the man. "Shh, darling. You'd best quiet down. Let me and your friend here finish our little transaction."

I've rarely ever seen her tears. She's not normally one to make them. Usually, I'm the one who needs comforting. Needs my eyes dried. And she's always the one to do it. Fearless Henriette. Well, Hen, today it's my turn. Today, I save you.

The man scowls; his voice grows sharper. "Hand it over, then. I won't ask twice." I nod, and I try to stay calm. I try to use it to lure him in. A false sense of security. "I'm just going to reach into my bag now," I tell him. He shakes his head. "Not so fast, friend." He takes a few steps, stopping an inch away from me, the barrel of his cannon in my face. "Let's keep any potential wrong moves to a minimum here, please." Then he nods for me to go ahead.

I'm absolutely relieved. He took the bait. And now he'll pay the price. I can't go just yet, though. I need just…one more glance. One last look at those eyes of hers. I can't help it.

It's too late now, anyway. My hand is in the bag, and I've already pulled the pin. No turning back. My eyes dart to the side, to hers. They lock, one last time. I'm at peace. I let her know with a smile. I hope she finds hers.

I swear she's in my head, hearing me say goodb—

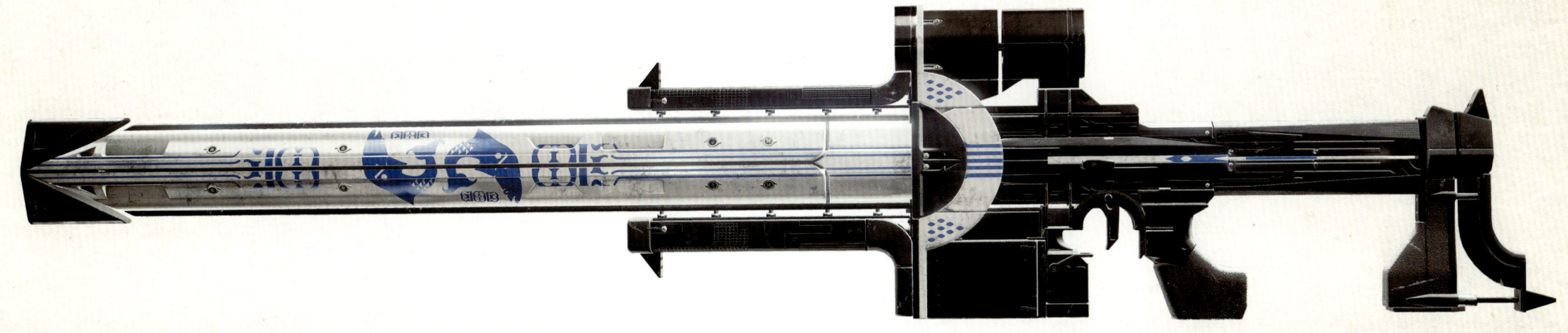

JÖTUNN

"Untamed. Destructive. As forceful and chaotic as Ymir himself."
—Ada-1

To: Henriette Meyrin

CC: Yuki Satou

Subject: Yesterday...

Hen,

It's no secret that our conversation yesterday didn't go as smoothly as it could have. I came in hot, and you overreacted. We'll both have to learn to be more professional in those kinds of situations going forward.

But I'm not just going to drop this. The Armory will be better for it. It's a chance to make real meaningful connections with organizations that want what we want. The possibilities are endless.

Look, you sought me out, brought me here to this project in large part, because of my connections. This is the gold mine. And I know I haven't said the best things about them in the past. Had my share of hiccups with them. They're not perfect, but then again, neither are we. What the Armory is doing, many would lump us both together.

I know that's not the best sales pitch, so let me put it in perspective: Enemy of my enemy. It's that simple. We're all preparing to fight the same threat, whatever it may be, and we all stand to lose the same things. Our best bet is to stand together, and we start that process here, one step at a time. Exos are the future. And we can help make them better than ever.

Plus, don't forget we hold the cards here. This is our tech. They can't touch it, modify it, etc., without our approval. But they can try and steal it or replicate it. I'd rather we maintain control of it—wouldn't you?

Listen—we're sisters. We're family. You know I love you, and you know I wouldn't come to you with this if I didn't think it wasn't in the Armory's best interests. And in all honesty, if you firmly decide no, then I'll respect that. You know I will.

But please say yes. For the future of the Armory. For the future of humanity. For the futures of our children.

—Helga

THE LAST WORD

"Yours, until the last flame dies and all words have been spoken."
—S<small>HIN</small> M<small>ALPHUR</small> <small>TO YOU, AS YOU JOURNEY FORTH INTO THE UNKNOWN</small>

Knew this day would come, and with it, one last lesson…

There's an end to all things, kid. Good and bad.

Sure, the best times seem small, and the bad tend to linger, but the only permanent is eternity.

I'm off to meet it.

If you're lucky, someday you will too.

For now, though, you've got road yet traveled and lives yet lived.

I know you got hate in you. Most do. Trick is to use it, 'stead of it usin' you.

But you know this—vengeance is a motivator, not the motive.

Meant to—hoped to—say these words to you one last time in person, but writin' 'em down seems the safe bet with the prey we're trackin'.

Worst part about bein' a good guy? As much as you may want it, you can't always win. But that truth don't bother me. We do the right thing, 'cause the right thing needs doin'. So, when another does harm—casts their shadow upon you or your kin—you go 'head and hunt for the justice needed to answer any sins inflicted.

Don't hunt 'em 'cause you been wronged.

Hunt 'em 'cause what they did was wrong.

There's a world of difference there, kid.

One makes you selfish. The other makes you a hero.

And I see a hero in you.

And with this last good lesson, a gift. I know it feels right in your hand—its weight easy, its trigger smooth. Use it as you will—I know you'll use it right.

It's yours now, 'til the last flame dies and all words've been spoken.

'Til that time.

Safe journeys. Straight aim. And good huntin'.

J.

—A letter to Shin Malphur from his third father, Jaren Ward, written before Ward's ill-fated showdown with the infamous Dredgen Yor in the wooded hollow beyond Beggars' Gulch

LE MONARQUE

"Wings flutter. Beauty distracts. Poison injects. The butterfly's curse extends to your enemies. A short life, shortened further by your hand."
—Ada-1

We sit together and stare out into the distance, at the mountains that stretch toward the heavens. There are still vibrant parts of the world, and we must not forget them. To fill her mind with them is to make her Human. To connect her to the world before.

Nearby, a flutter of butterflies seek their next batch of sustenance, knowing not what the world around them has become.

She watches them. They are new to her. A wayward butterfly from the flutter lands on her arm. She looks at it, and then to me. "Le Monarque," she says. I nod and attempt a smile. I watch her. Somehow she reminds me of it. Beautiful and dangerous all at once.

Sadness washes over me. I reach out and rub her back, a fleeting moment of comfort for us both, as the feel of her cold body against my hand causes me to pull away. For a moment, I forgot what she was.

There's an awkward silence. I steal another glance at her, simultaneously frightened of and in awe of who and what she is.

A product of my own twisted ambition and desperation.

The monarch flies away, unlikely to be seen again.

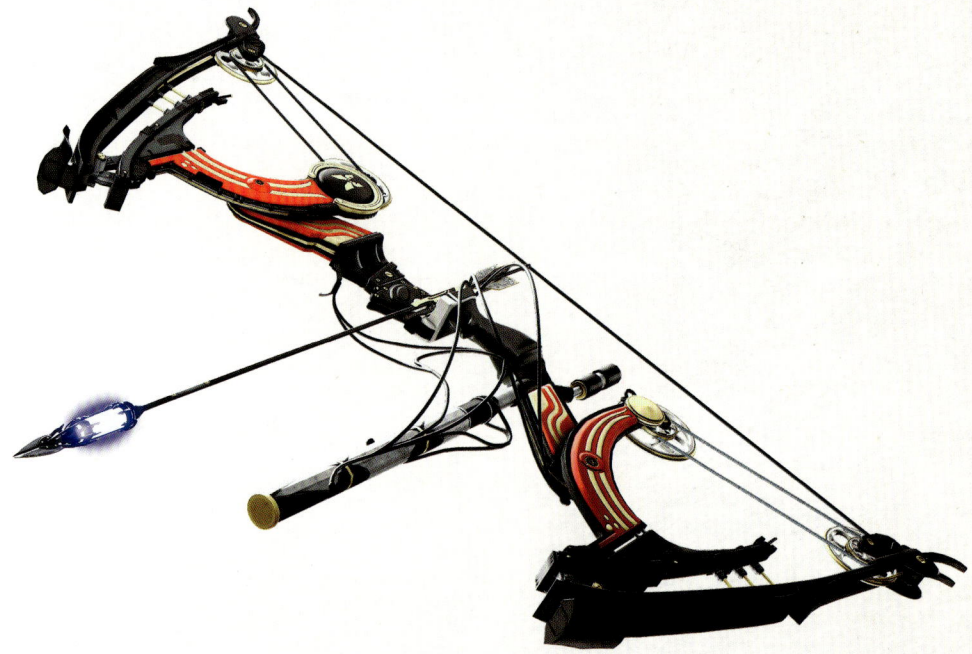

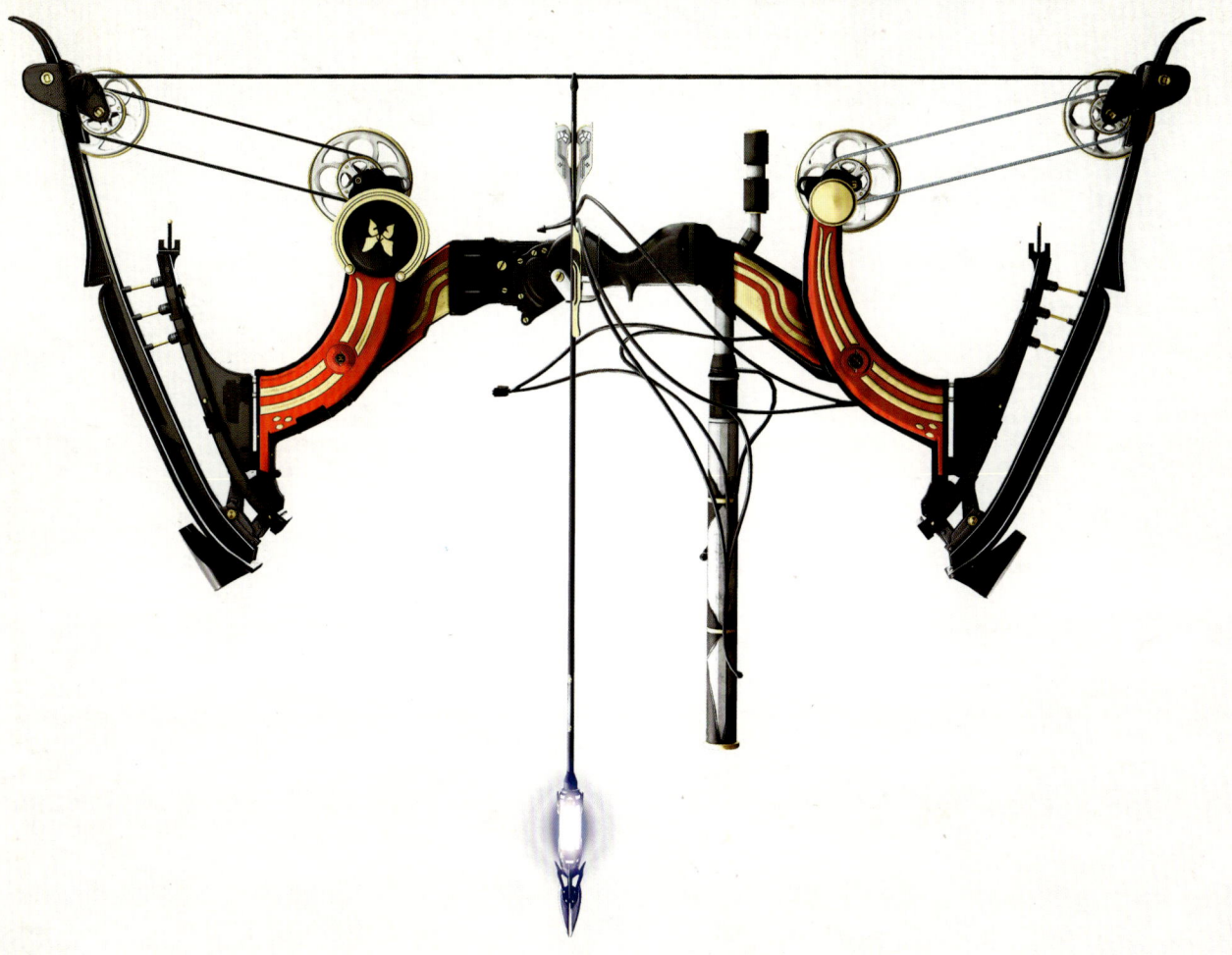

Season 6

SEASON OF THE DRIFTER

The Drifter upped the ante on his Gambit, much to the Vanguard's disappointment. The Guardian made a choice—to spy on the Drifter, or to work more closely with him.

The Guardian learned bits of the Drifter's past: that the Nine are patrons of his endeavors, and that he knew their Emissary in days past, when both were different people.

ARBALEST

"We didn't have linear fusions in the Dark Age. But we made it work." —The Drifter

"Nah. Dark Age version was better."

"You and I remember the Dark Age differently."

"I'll take a hard projectile over energy any day. No better way to make sure the target is dead."

"Energy is for silencing barriers. Fists are all I need to administer blunt-force trauma."

"I forget you used to be a Warlord."

"What do you mean, 'used to'?"

"I thought you'd thrown in with Saladin and Felwinter."

"I did. But I never stopped being me."

"Then why—"

"'Warlord' is too many syllables."

"Gambit needs more candidates like you. Should stop by sometime. Whatever you want to call yourself."

"Thank you. You're a liar and a cheat. Stay out of my Crucible."

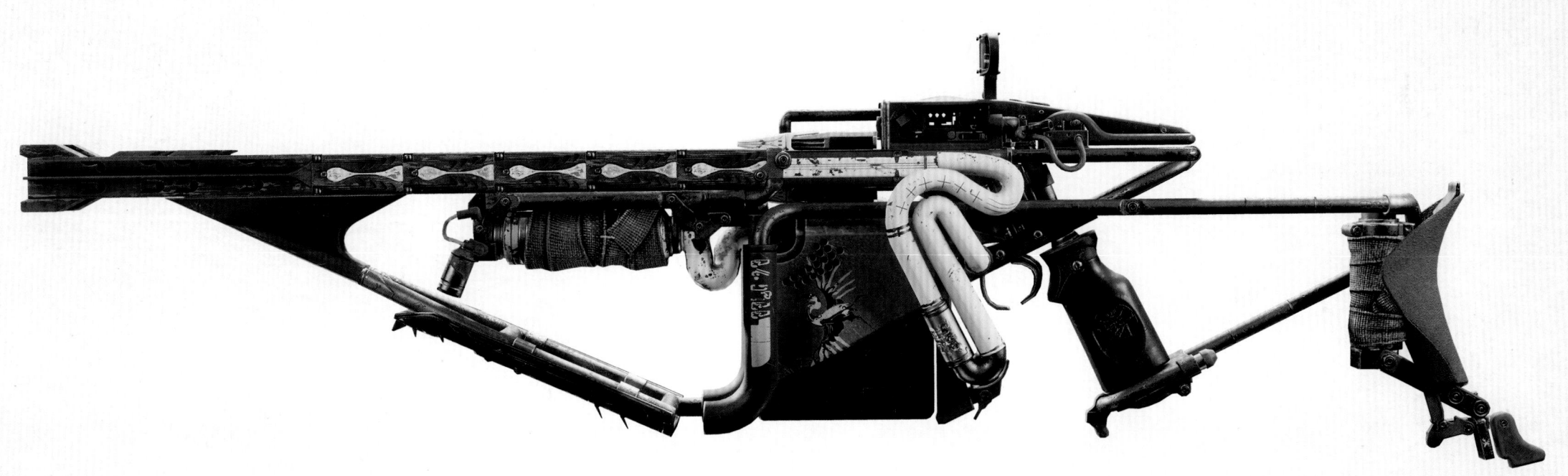

THORN

"To rend one's enemies is to see them not as equals, but as objects—hollow of spirit and meaning."
—13th Understanding, 7th Book of Sorrow

"The Weapons of Sorrow are not the endgame, but a road map. Each evolution, every advance in the delivery of pain and the mastery of destruction, feeds the Hive's hateful weapons research. They will map every scream, harness every aggression, until they understand every method by which to ravage the hearts, minds, and flesh of humanity. And in doing so, they will turn us against ourselves—feeding our lust, our greed, our fear until we become a threat unto ourselves like none we could imagine. So, wield these, angry reaper. Strive to know the darkness in your own heart. Walk in the shadows of fallen heroes. And know that you are an enemy of hope."

—A warning

OUTBREAK PERFECTED

~directive=KILL while enemies=PRESENT: execute(directive)~

The Captain stands with his primary hands braced on a command table. He stares down at a static holoprojection as though it might reveal some new secret. Nearby, the Hunter combs through scout reports. The Warlock taps rapidly at a datapad, running simulation after simulation. No one speaks.

There is a deafening boom. The holoprojection flickers; the whole Skiff tilts seventy degrees off-kilter. The Captain holds tight to the table, reaching out with a secondary arm to snatch the Hunter as he goes toppling by. The Warlock is not a concern; she has Blinked her way to a secure handhold.

The Captain calls to his crew, speaking Eliksni too fast for the Hunter or the Warlock to follow. Someone calls back. The Skiff tilts nauseously, then stabilizes.

"Eramis?" the Warlock asks.

The Captain nods. Letting go of the Hunter, he disappears through an access hatch to consult with his crew.

"I don't like this," the Hunter says quietly. "We should be there with him."

The Warlock chews on her lower lip. She doesn't like it either, but they've argued endlessly with their Captain and gained no ground. "We have to trust him," she says finally. "This is what he wants."

"Trust him to die?" the Hunter hisses. "Let's break down how stupid this is: Not only does he wants to infiltrate the Tower without us, he's also planning to wear Devils colors to interrupt a Devils heist to reclaim SIVA. And instead of leaning on us, his good Guardian friends, he's banking on some stranger—"

"Not a stranger," the Warlock cuts in.

"Fine! Not a stranger, but definitely not a friend!" The Hunter grits his teeth. "We should do it. We need to do it. Let's just go; let's go now. We can cut them off." He conjures his Ghost with a twist of his wrist, readying for transmat.

"We have to trust him," the Warlock repeats, reaching out to grasp the Hunter's forearm. "I think he's right when he says it doesn't mean anything if we do it. Guardians do extraordinary things all the time. And he needs more allies..."

The Captain reenters their little ad hoc war room. They draw up guiltily. The Hunter hides his Ghost.

"All well?" he asks, looking between them.

"Eia, Mithrax," the Warlock murmurs. "We're all good."

The Hunter says nothing.

"We walk this hardship path with joyful hearts. Be brave."

Season 7

SEASON OF OPULENCE

Emperor Calus, disgraced former leader of the Cabal, enticed the Guardian back to his Leviathan ship with promises of power, all in the hopes that he could sway them to his clandestine ranks as a Shadow.

The Guardian competed in Calus's Menagerie and claimed their spoils, but their allegiances remained steadfast.

BAD JUJU

"If you believe your weapon wants to end all existence, then so it will." —Toland the Shattered

Hello again, my trenchant Dante.

You have stepped in and out of sharp-edged worlds, hewn gods into blunt fractions, twinned yourself with powers whose names cannot even be held in the language of little gray cells. You think yourself very high up on the pyramid of contumely.

If you only knew how high that pyramid goes.

Higher than I knew when my radiant killer unsung me from biological squalor, or when I witnessed a royal secret turn death into a chrysalis. Higher than I described in my journals, or told to our mutual three-eyed friend.

Higher than even I, sailor upon the Sea of Screams that I am, can yet see.

Perhaps I will tell you about them.

You are right to ask why I would do so. Very good, dear squanderer—your intentions have grown sharp as thrallteeth.

You see, they know. What you are, what you were, what you will become. They know.

What lean tithes you are to them. Soft whetstones make for dull blades.

This I define as the truth and tension of the rope: To bind, one must apply force at both ends.

I think perhaps I will tell you after all.

TRUTH

"… is where you seek it." —L<small>OMAR</small>

Smoke winds away from the battlefield in wavering scarves.

Corsairs and Crows move through the wreckage in pairs, searching for their dead. When they find Awoken survivors, they call for help. When they find a Devil or a Wolf, they call for a field medic and prison-grade restraints.

A Vandal watches all of this from the wing of a Galliot with his four arms folded around his knees. He knows battle, and so death does not disturb him. He was born of war, made for it, shaped by it. And yet, as he stares out at the charred bodies of his cousins, at the bent bodies of his new allies…

"Vel," Sjur says, startling him. He peers down to find her on tiptoes, chin on the edge of the Galliot's wing. She juts her thumb over her shoulder, indicating the battlefield. "Npariimoqilum?"

He frowns. "Res kaqilum? Psekisk."

She frowns back at him, and though she only has two eyes, her stare is mother-strong.

The Vandal sighs and lets go of his knees. "Variisis," he grumbles as he slides off the Galliot, skulking past her.

"Ha ha," she replies, humorless.

He picks his way down to the worst of it and joins the search. Over the next hour, he finds a Wolf that he half-remembers from a distant relative's coming-of-age ceremony; three Devils who look at him with uncomprehending confusion and anger; and one Crow irretrievably trapped beneath the fuselage of his ship.

He is about to abandon a ruined Devils Skiff when he hears a faint hiss from inside a ventilation shaft. He clambers up to peer into its grate and sees four wary eyes shining back at him.

A hatchling, still soft and translucent with its egg-molt.

Carefully, he pries the grate open and beckons to her. "Velask, kelekh," he murmurs. "Nankemrak."

She crawls into his palm and his heart surges.

LUMINA

There must be meaning in my roar.

In young languages, we sketched for each other the seemings of stars and planets and the black between galaxies.

We have devoted ourselves to listening. To the Cosmos, by crafting assemblers that can translate for us the mechanical language of Order. And to our own withins, by withstanding the howling storm until patience and humility made of chaos—if not sense, then at least peace.

From beyond emptiness, a Gardener emerged, drawn from pseudophotons and impossible math. And our nest of colliding space dust was never the same.

For it heard meaning in our roar.

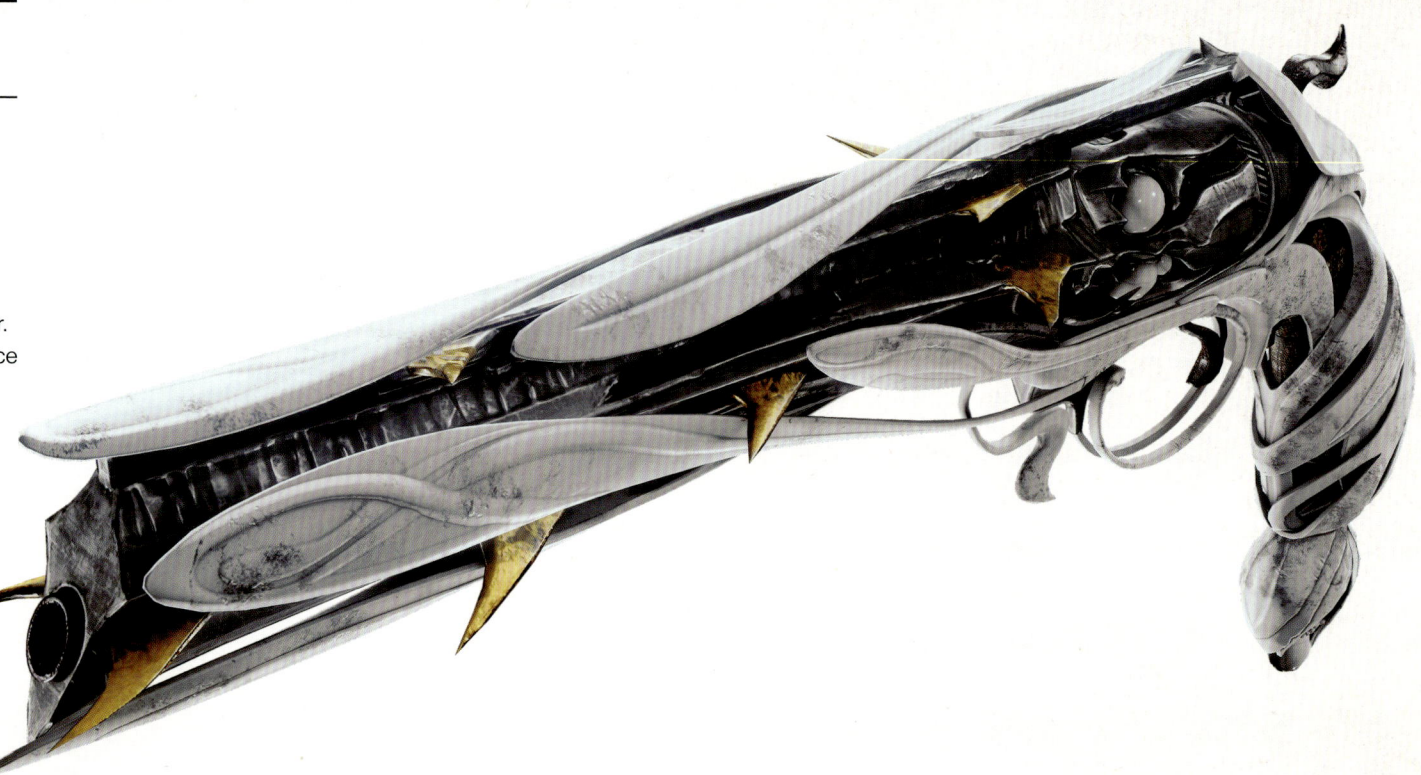

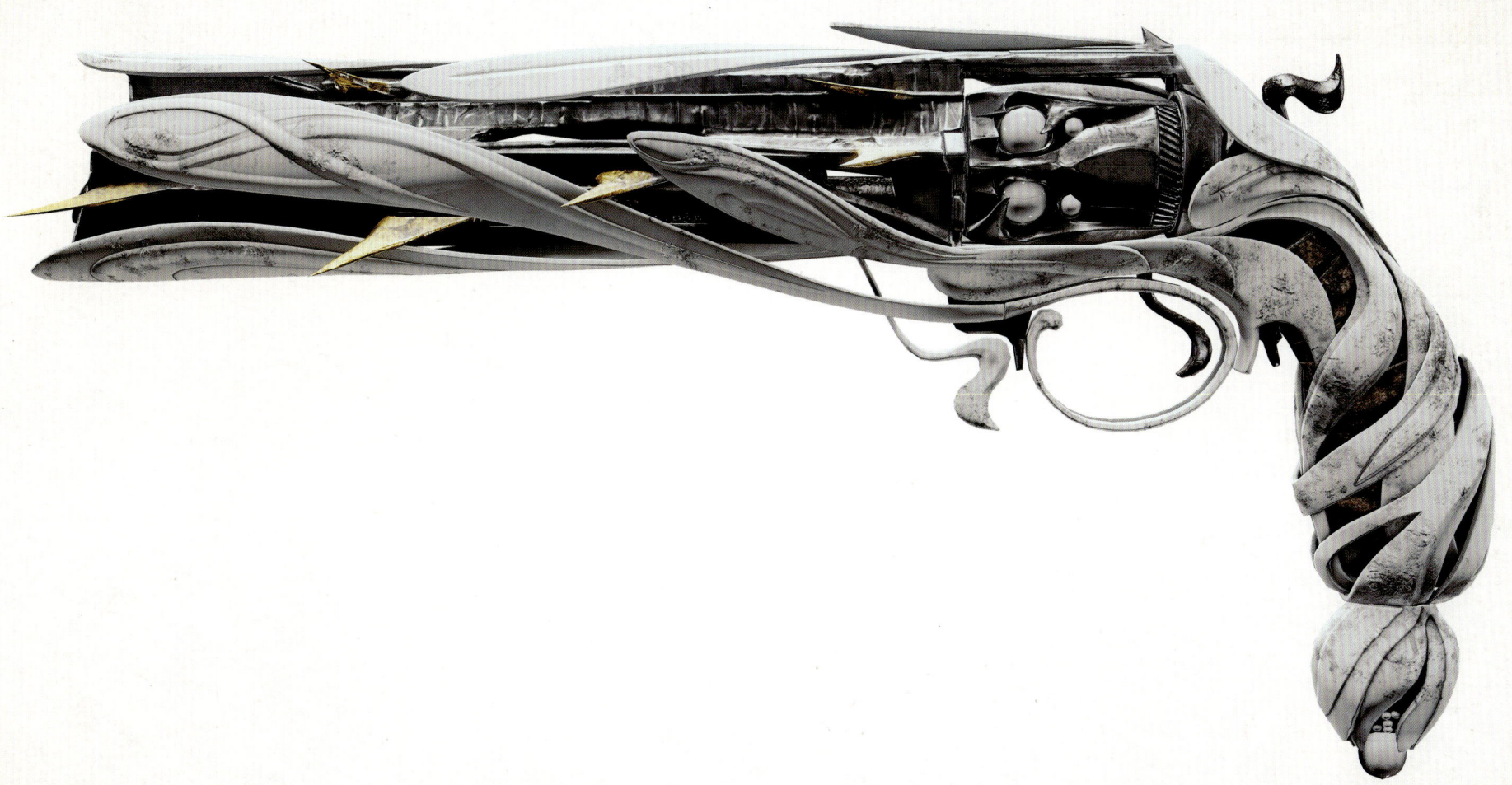

TARRABAH

We walk where our ancestors once walked.

The world is very big again.

It used to be small. I know because I was born inside its commwire-satellite-datawave skeleton.

But even before that, before the Traveler wove us into a tapestry of peculiar threads, this was a planet of big, big worlds.

Many of those worlds were lost in a collapse, but not the one you're thinking of. Before the great Collapse, there was another. A longer, slower, bitterer collapse.

Some things survive. Names upon rusted signs, phrases in impervious microfiche. As other Guardians save Humans, I save words. I save stories.

That is my mission, here on the shores of the Hawkesbury Sea. I surface the survivors. The sweet-voiced koodelong. The swift gangurru. The sharp-fanged tarrabah.

It's a mission the Traveler started. After all, she surfaced me.

Season 8

SHADOWKEEP – SEASON OF THE UNDYING

The Vex, spurred by the reactivation of the Pyramid on Earth's Moon, opened a portal to the Black Garden. Their forces spewed forth, assaulting the lunar surface.

Ikora Rey and the Guardian launched offensives into the Garden, using a portal of Ikora's creation to track and destroy the Vex leader: the Undying Mind. The Guardian recovered a relic of Darkness from within the Garden.

DEATHBRINGER

"Sing them a lullaby of death and nothing more."

"The Song is the antithesis. The Song is destruction. The failure to master the harmonies of life has birthed the anti-creation—the sullen frequencies of ruin. Those sweet melodies carry with them more than death—a rending of spirit and mind, a flaying of the physical self till nothing remains.

"The beauty of the cascading notes. The imperfect inflection of their tune… there has ever been, and will ever be, art in creation. So too in the act of annihilation—erasure and bittersweet finality. This is the Song's truest gift…

"In its wake, once the echoes have rung their last, there is only silence and the grand splendor of nothingness.

"Thus is the Song an end, and those who join its Choir are death, and nothing more."

—Unknown

ERIANA'S VOW

A light in the dark.

Omar: This place reeks of death.

Toland: Worse. Rebirth.

Sai: Once something is gone, it should stay that way.

Eriana-3: I can't share that sentiment.

Sai: You will never find peace if you can't accept your loss.

Eriana-3: I'll find peace when I rip that monster's beating heart from his chest.

Eris: I have never known vengeance to bring peace.

Eriana-3: What do you think I should hope for, then? All I have left is my vengeance and my gun.

Eris: A hand cannon with a sight, yet you see nothing but rage. Don't allow it to cloud your judgment. Wei gave you the weapon for a purpose.

Eriana-3: Yeah, to keep me at a distance from the Hive. And now I'm heading straight toward them. Somewhere out there, she's shaking a fist at me.

Eris: We can honor her still by ridding the world of the disease that is Crota.

Eriana-3: There is no world for me after Crota.

Eris: What you are feeling . . . is to be expected. In time, we can forge a new world. Together.

Eriana-3: I want to believe that is possible.

Vell: I hate to interrupt this touching moment, but does anyone else hear that?

Sai: That rumble?

Toland: Thralls . . . I think they mean to welcome us.

Eriana-3: Let them come. I'll be the last Light they ever see.

DIVINITY

Calibrate reality. Seek inevitability. Embody divinity.

Lisbon-13 looked back toward where they'd left Yardarm-4. Separating the team always felt wrong, but Rekkana needed uninterrupted time to confer with the Senior Sybil, and if the Vex had detected their crash landing in the Black Garden, Yardarm-4 would give them that time.

"You'll have to move quickly," the Sybil said to Rekkana. Lisbon-13 shared her secret channel; Rekkana trusted him. "The Vanguard have discovered that our order persists, as Osiris predicted."

"They'll send a fireteam after us, then."

"And after any other Cryptochrons they learn of. But your path is more dangerous than most. The Circle has foreseen many fireteams following in your footsteps. You can find the knowledge the order seeks at the Tree."

"Can? Not will?" For the first time, Rekkana sounded concerned.

"The Circle has had limited success in piercing the veil that surrounds the Black Garden, so the order offers no certainties. They say that a group of Guardians will discover secrets about the origin of the Black Garden at the Tree. The Oneiromantic Circle foresees no reason why it will not be the Kentarch 3."

"Nor can I. But . . . ?"

"There is another thread in the tapestry, entwined with this one. The Vex, or some fractal faction of them, worship or honor a . . . divinity there."

"The Black Heart? It was destroyed."

"Yes, but this is something different. An object. Something like a sacred relic. It is important to the Vex for reasons that we have not yet fathomed. The Circle has determined that it is dangerous—"

"A Vex weapon?"

"Perhaps," the Sybil sounded annoyed at the interruption. "Rekkana, the Circle concluded that it is a danger to you."

"To me? But then, why send me on this mission?"

"When the Circle dreamed of the object, you were beside it."

"All right. We'll see what fate we will find ourselves in. Sybil . . . " Rekkana paused a long while. "I don't know that we'll see each other again."

"The veil around the Black Garden, the influence of the Vex—they make such matters difficult to know. I choose to believe we will meet again."

"Then I won't say goodbye," Rekkana said and closed the channel.

Rekkana stood, eyes closed, for a time. Lisbon-13 waited.

"Lisbon, when we find it," she said, opening her eyes, "you should carry it."

"The object? This divinity?"

"I can think of no one whom I'd trust more with it than you."

LEVIATHAN'S BREATH

"Cast a Shadow over the wilds of this universe. Return with glorious trophies." —EMPEROR CALUS

Don't ask me where I heard this—I honestly can't remember—but legend has it this bow has fouled more behemoths and seen more of the known universe than the whole Vanguard combined. You hear a lot of stories when you work as a Gunsmith as long as I have, and this bow has a wild one. This thing is the king of killers. Almost got Ghaul too. I think it was, um, Calus, who had it crafted for his huntsmaster—what's her name? Voyc? Yeah.

Anyway, Calus had this obsession with collecting the hides and heads of the rarest and most formidable creatures Voyc could find. And with this bow, she was real good at it. Gwern, the Unbeatable—defeated. Giant sea monsters—taken down to size. I even heard she slayed an Ahamkara, which is very impressive if it's true.

Calus was so thrilled with her that she got a promotion. Of sorts. It wasn't common knowledge. He called her "the Shadow of the Wilds," which never sat right with me. Psion Flayers aren't known for their stealth. She was his assassin. When she wasn't hunting prize game, she was doing Calus's dirty work in the most remote corners of the galaxy.

When Ghaul attacked the Tower, Calus thought this would be the perfect time to strike and ordered Voyc to do Ghaul in. Take a guess how that worked out. Makes you wonder who got to her first, 'cause with this bow in her hand, she shouldn't have failed. I'd like to attribute this to user error, 'cause when I found the bow near her corpse, it was still in pristine condition. I'm glad I grabbed it before the Tower was evacuated. Could all just be hearsay, but there's a real chance to vindicate this work of art and give it a legacy worth preserving. Hunting is fine, but Guardians have a greater purpose.

—Banshee-44

MONTE CARLO

There will always be paths to tread and methods to try. Roll with it.

"The math isn't the thing. The math is an inside joke. Just old solutions some say hint at the pinnacle of pre–Golden Age thought mechanics. My partner used to go on about it. About probabilities and random patterns used to solve the unsolvable. I never really paid attention. Outdated science never equaled a good payday, if you follow.

"Anyway, we used to run resource grabs along a coast out east. We found the rifle in the ruins of a gamblin' hall. In a vault ten feet thick. Behind glass, like it was someone's somethin' special—a real showpiece. Thought for sure we had a solid score. Funny bit was, the spot where we found it . . . ? It was named after the math. Or, that's what my partner said. My money says the opposite, but what I know about science and history is limited to what I can sell and the sum it'll fetch.

"So, we're out in that ruined hall with loot to spare and an old-time shooter that should trade for a small fortune. Then scavengers hit. Small crew, but mean. My partner took bolts. Dropped. I tried to cover him, but the pirates were on us.

"Last I saw, his Ghost got scraped by a line rifle. Nothing I could do. Only reason me and my girl made it out was she was off scoutin' our escape, and I . . . the Fallen were distracted by my partner. But, I'm tellin' ya . . . there was nothing I could do."

"You were lucky to make it back—with your life, and your 'treasure.'"

"You could say that."

"You survived an unauthorized run in known Fallen territory. You found an advanced Golden Age firearm with functional tech in a sealed chamber. You sold the weapon's tech to a gunsmith you won't name for a 'small fortune' in Glimmer. And your partner is nowhere to be found—'dead by Fallen hands'—so that 'fortune' is all yours. No need to split it."

"Sure. When you look at it that way, the math ain't so bad."

—Egon Bash, a questionable Hunter under Vanguard interrogation

XENOPHAGE

This might sting a little.

There was only darkness... until there was Light. Again. A third time.

I knew it. Knew I'd be back one day—only this time, I was something else. Something... not Human. Not by choice, of course. Those damn Hive. They weren't just tryin' to kill me. They were using me to get to my Light. To drain it from my soul. For their sick experiments.

But the idiots screwed up. They didn't just drain my Light. They took the whole lot. The entire thing. Soul and all. I'm still me. I'm just not the me I knew. The one with two arms and two legs. I'm something smaller now.

But honestly, it's no bother. The fire inside me... it came too. And it rages now more than ever before. The fools have no clue what they've done. No idea the price they'll pay.

I'll have my vengeance. In this life, not the next.

—Omar Agah

Season 9

SEASON OF DAWN

Osiris exited the Infinite Forest with a portent of humanity's doom, foreseen in the simulations. He learned the remains of the Red Legion had taken the Sundial, a failed time-travel experiment of his own invention.

The Guardian fought the Cabal and their Psion Council to stop them from rewriting history, then used the same methods to save the lost Guardian Saint-14 from his death in the past.

BASTION

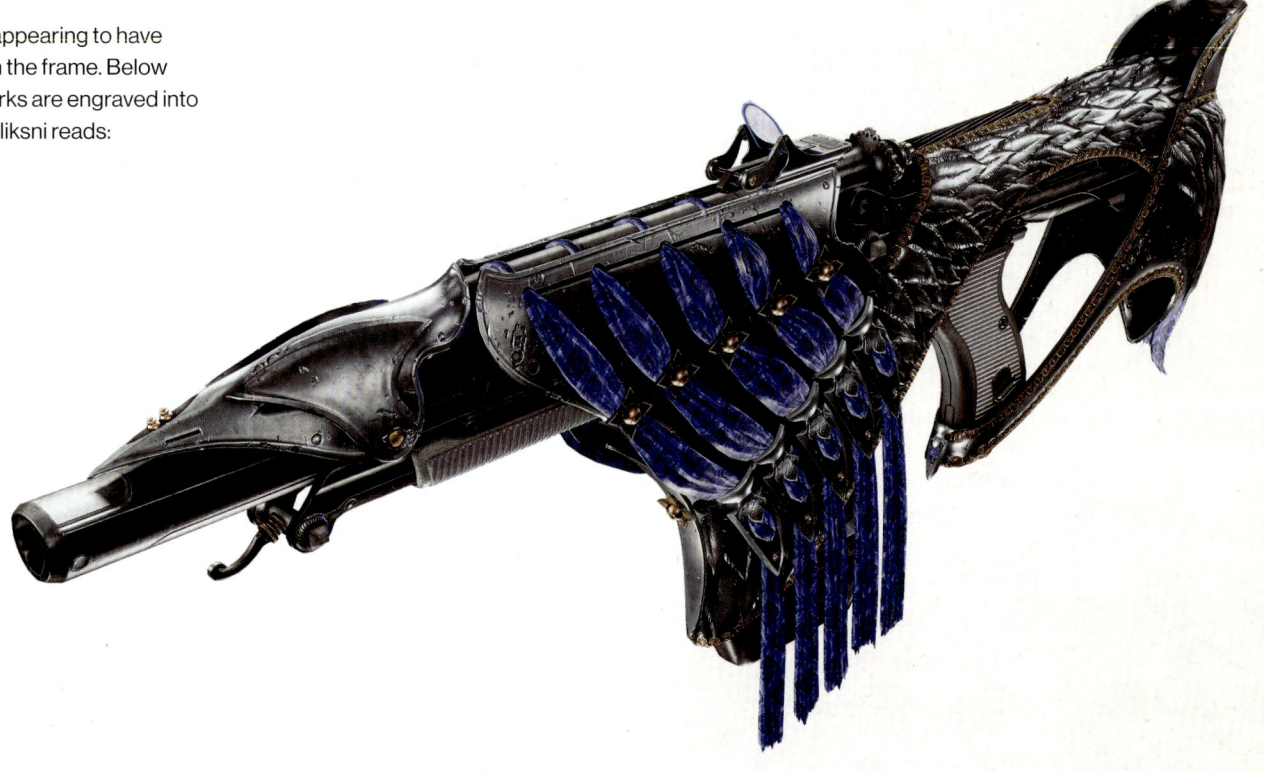

"The final stand is wherever I plant my feet. Not one step more." —Saint-14

My son.

You are a bastion of hope for all who are lost in darkness.

Let this consecrated armament offer protection in times of trial,

strength when you feel most alone,

and guidance when there are no roads.

Your Light will shine on to lead our people into peace.

Let this be a symbol of our dedication to their future.

Know that I am proud.

—Father

The epitaph is barely readable, appearing to have been scraped almost clean from the frame. Below the stricken words, five hash marks are engraved into the weapon. A small etching in Eliksni reads:

|||||

"Dead . . . little . . . thieves . . ."

DEVIL'S RUIN

"Press on! The Devils will rue the day they came to our doors!" —Lord Shaxx

"There is a reason we fight. It's not simply the thrill of battle. There are those who depend on us to stand up, hold the line, and defend what we hold dear. The battle for Twilight Gap remains the hallmark for our fortitude and a prominent reminder that nothing we do is easy.

"I recall Shaxx defiantly ignoring Saladin's orders to fall back, driving his fireteam to a final push on the wall of the Last City. It ended up providing the momentum we needed to save the City, but also splintered bonds between the Titans. Perhaps I can help suture these wounds, now that I have returned.

"Even so, our memories are flooded by moments of pain, duress, and strife. Use them. Wield them. Channel them through you.

"Carry a piece of the battle with you.

"While this will never replace the mighty Gjallarhorns of old, glory comes in all sizes, and we can still celebrate the victory at the Gap with munitions such as these. It is more than a gun. It is a symbol. Each component of this weapon represents a sacrifice made for the greater good. May it bring you the strength to prevail when all looks lost.

"Should the City ever come under threat again, you'll be ready."

—Saint-14

SYMMETRY

"Duality is not a curse, but a gift." —Author unknown

"The road ahead is unknown, but time tells us many things. The moments that become past in turn become blueprints for the future. In this space, there is no right or wrong.

"We find a contemporaneous merging of what is known and what is unknown here. Somewhere between the knowns and unknowns lies the real. The tangible.

"There is a weight to it—a feeling that tells you what you hold is true.

"But what if the truth hasn't been told? What if the truth is a lie?

"New paths present themselves. Blueprints change. We walk the line of truth every day.

"But now, the line that holds the gentle balance has been crossed.

"The truth is, this won't be the last time."

—Excerpt from the Symmetry pamphlet "A Place Between"

Season 10

SEASON OF THE WORTHY

With their plans for the Sundial foiled, the Legion made a desperate play for revenge on humanity. They launched the derelict *Almighty*, former pride of Ghaul's fleet, at the Last City.

Ana Bray and the Vanguard put aside their differences and made a plan to use Rasputin's Warsat network to neutralize the threat. The Guardian powered Rasputin's arsenal, and the Warmind destroyed the *Almighty*.

THE FOURTH HORSEMAN

It's not a holdout weapon; it's a pathfinder.

"There's a reason the Cabal want to take this weapon from us.

"When you hold the Fourth Horseman in your hands, you bring the storm. You instill fear by commanding the thunder and firing off rounds with lightning speed. Tear through your enemies like light piercing through clouds after the rain subsides.

"You are a force of nature. Unstoppable. Unpredictable. Undeniable.

"Don't forget what the Fourth Horseman brings, after all."

—Commander Zavala

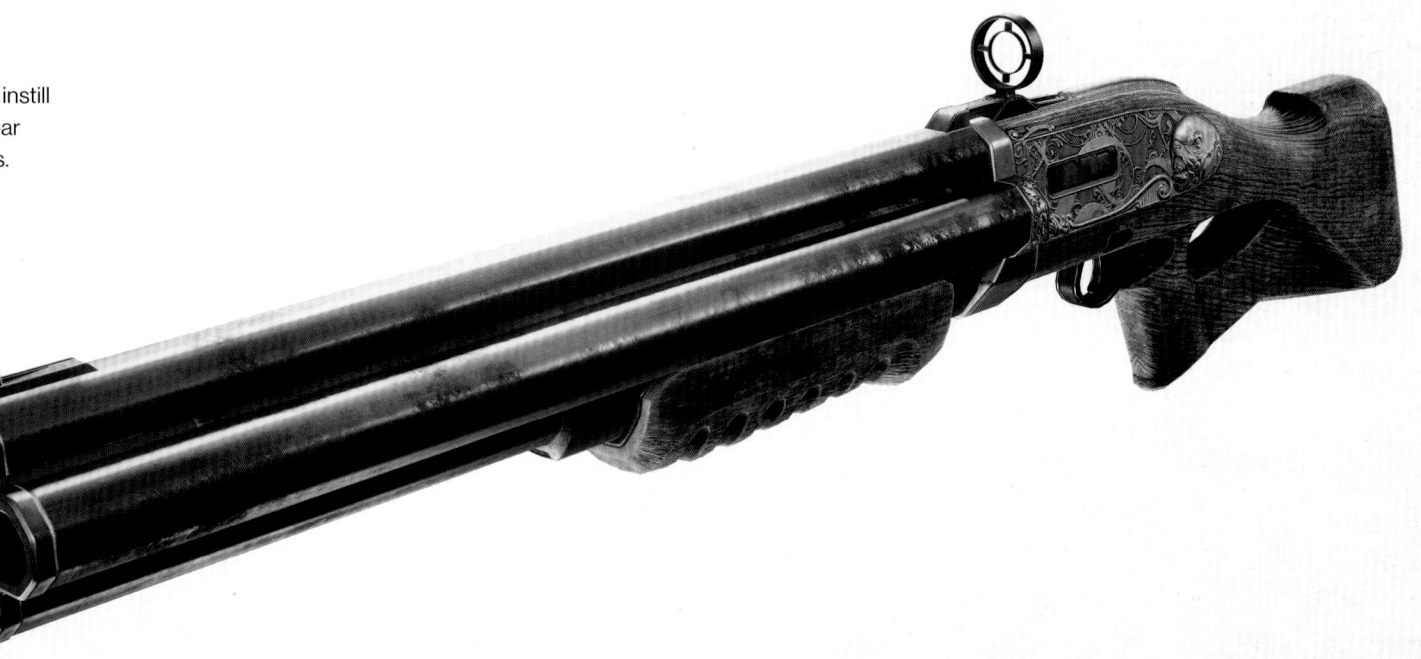

TOMMY'S MATCHBOOK

"It's warm in here."

The entrance to the Hunter's den on 7th Street immediately led to a flight of dark, dirty steps that went down two stories and multiple flights. A maglev train roared overhead as Aunor reached the bottom. She had blinked through the Void to skip as many steps as she could. It made her a little angry. The Hunters who built this place must have thought the stairs were theatrical and intimidating instead of a complete waste of time.

Like this trip was turning out to be. The place was deserted. No one had passed her on the way down. Multiple card tables sat under a single rusty overhead lamp. There were a few possibly loaded sidearms left on the floor and rifles leaning against the walls. The occasional food wrapper from the deli upstairs accompanied the guns on the floor. There were more guns by far.

Something moved in the corner.

Aunor's Minuet-42 hand cannon came up in her fist.

"Hey, whoa. No one draws in the den. Are you crazy?"

A Hunter in full strike gear and his Ghost walked out of the shadows, hands and shell pieces in the air. It was the Ghost who had spoken. "Oh, a Warlock. That tracks."

The Hunter looked on in silence.

Aunor flashed her Cormorant Seal. "Aunor, Praxic Order."

"What does internal affairs want with a Hunter den?" The question itself was a lie.

"Your names."

"I'm Tommy," said the Ghost.

"I'm Ghost," said the Hunter.

Aunor holstered the Minuet, made another visual sweep of the room. "Where is everyone? Hunters have been hard to find in the Tower. Bounties and strike assignments are piling up."

Tommy cocked his shell. "The Drifter must have the Praxics working overtime. Since Cayde died—"

Ghost drew a long knife across the back of his armored fist. It sang coldly.

"—every single Hunter worth their salt is either out on a mission to save the world or spending their time away from the City. To avoid the Vanguard Dare."

Aunor looked from Ghost to Tommy and back again.

"Listen," Tommy whispered, as Ghost sheathed his knife and stepped forward. He held out a long, white-bodied rifle with a flat, disc-shaped drum instead of a standard magazine. "This is the most expensive thing we own. You can have it. Just please don't tell anyone we were here. And get someone in that Vanguard chair. The Hunters are losing their minds out there."

HEIR APPARENT

"The Red Legion will march again." —Caiatl

Caiatl stands in her war room.

Her nation, which she has always loved, reeks of failure. The scent is strong. When she was young, she would watch the feedings in her father's zoological gardens. Live creatures from the lands beyond Torobatl, wounded, left in the middle of the landscaped enclosures. She'd seen how the smell of blood brought the larger, hungrier creatures out of the undergrowth. The same will happen to the empire if she lets it.

But she will not.

She won't fail where her father failed. He was led astray by his vices, corrupted by frivolity and pleasure. He was never meant to be emperor; he was too weak. But Ghaul was destroyed by weakness, too. His fixation on the machine god was stupid. It embarrasses her to think of him.

She has always had a vivid imagination. Ironically, it's her father she can thank for that—all of the stories and songs he made her study, the insufferable plays. But she repurposes that arsenal of thought toward a new goal: imagining a better future for her people. A future where they rule the galaxy once again, where foreign ships fall under their fire and rival nations fall to their knees. This future will be different.

This future will be hers.

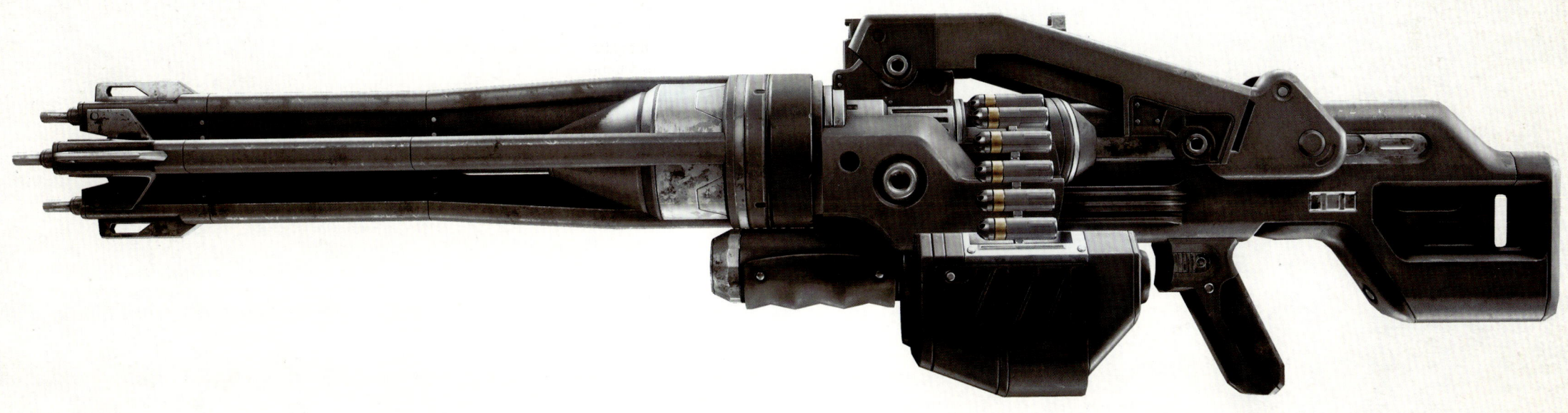

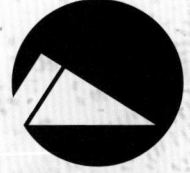

Season 11

SEASON OF ARRIVALS

The Black Fleet, humanity's ancient foe, returned to our system and knocked out Rasputin's defenses with trivial ease. The Vanguard evacuated some stellar bodies as the Pyramids descended on them.

The Guardian worked with Eris Morn to translate cryptic messages from the Pyramids while battling back the enemies of humanity, now emboldened by the growing shadow enveloping humanity.

RUINOUS EFFIGY

From the many wings of ruin blows a wind that will reshape this dead world.

"That's not right."

Banshee-44 taps a spectral analyzer against the Effigy's frame.

Commander Zavala turns, closes the lid on a small golden weapon case, and walks to Banshee's side. "What have you found?"

"Well, it's not petrified wood, but it is organic."

"That's troubling," Zavala says as he moves to run his fingers over the weapon's frame.

"I wouldn't."

A shallow cold saps the heat from Zavala's fingertips; he pulls back. "This wasn't in Eris's report." His voice is thin and stark with disappointment, as if spoken through dead winter air.

"Guardian doesn't seem to notice either." Banshee clinks the analyzer into a tool tray. "Leeches a bit, kicks out Void. Sig's hazy, though. Wild."

Long quiet overtakes the workshop, imposed by shuttered windows and empty streets below.

They stand over the weapon. Banshee stares down and nods along to the ambient static.

"What were you saying?" The weapon master's voice is framed in apology.

Zavala puts a hand on Banshee's shoulder, smiles, and gestures to the weapon. "Equipment that uses the wielder's Light is not unprecedented."

"It doesn't use it; it eats it. Thing's got an appetite. Works almost like, uh . . . a converter."

"Is it dangerous?"

"Nah. Guardian doesn't even seem to notice. I'll get you a write-up."

SEASON 11: Season of Arrivals

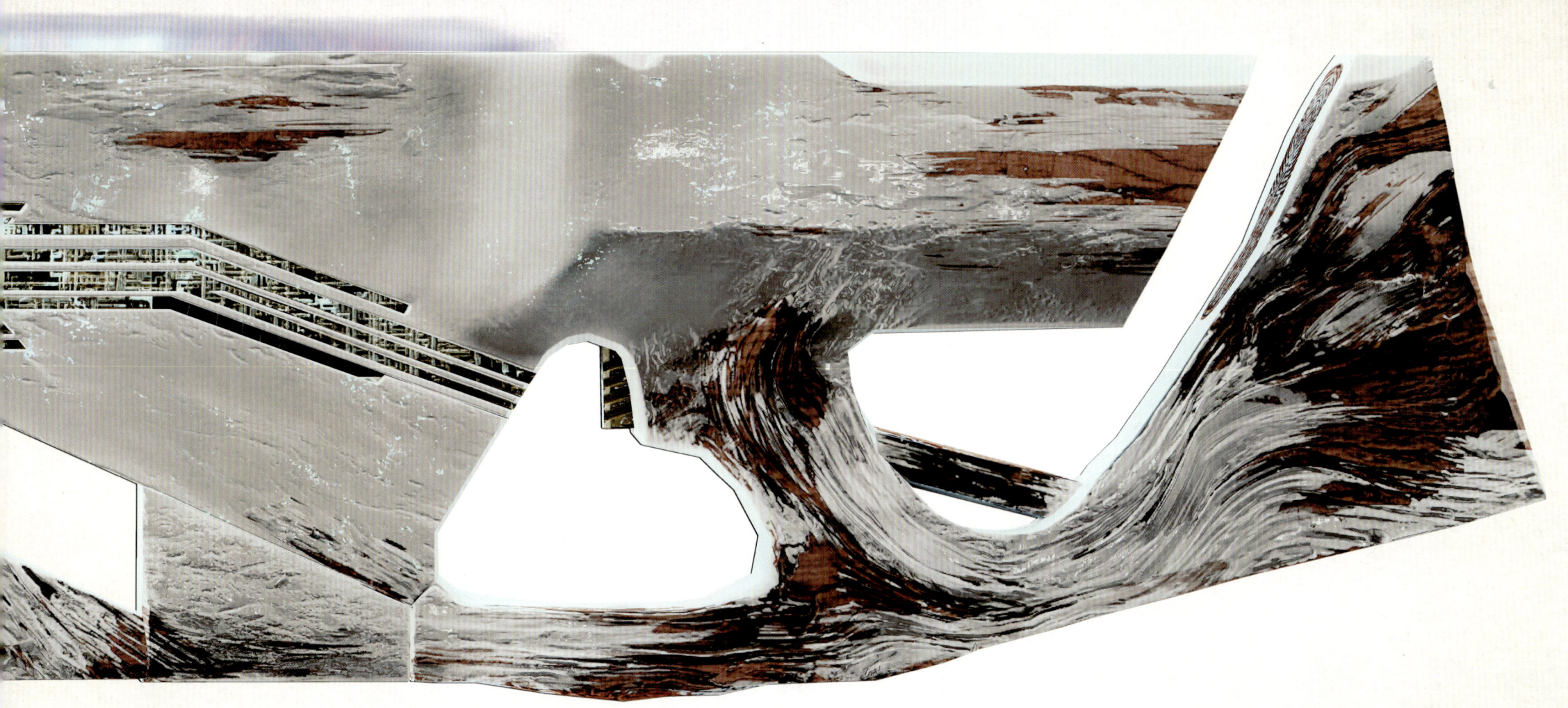

TRAVELER'S CHOSEN

"All we have left now is our faith."

I push into my ossific, den and he is there.

I see him looking over the side, toward his Traveler, head bent. He is speaking softly, but I can hear him. Anyone who was listening could.

He waits for a response, and I do as well, tense, curious. He stands attentively, this loyal dog of a man. It is no time at all for me, but for him, the hours creep by in silence.

I am ready to choke the voice of his Traveler if it answers him, but there is nothing. He tightens his grip on the railing.

I feel something shift inside him, and a new possibility presents itself.

*

Again, I press against the sockets. The net creaks softly with my eagerness.

Someone approaches, and he turns his back to his Traveler. There is an exchange, obscured by the rubicund thrash.

He is given reports. Hope bleeds from him. He gives the messenger a token of his faith. They accept it without understanding its meaning.

He watches as they leave. There is a hollow place in his center. It is beautiful.

*

I return warily.

I do not see him, but I hear him. He speaks to all with a voice thick with grief.

I must learn how far I have been set back. I reach to him tentatively. Strength. I push—and feel only sweet, soft rot.

I am delirious with pleasure. It gave them no answers; it was a reflex, the spasm of dumb muscle.

A song of joy rises within me.

Now.

WITHERHOARD

"Like a one-man private security company." —THE DRIFTER

The Drifter slouches against the bulkhead of the *Derelict*, a pile of Dark Motes scattered across the table in front of him. He fixes his gaze on the massive Titan, the sharpness in his eyes belying his casual posture.

"I'm surprised you got the time to come around here, hassling me about these tiny Motes, Joxer. Seems like you got the big deal in orbit around Io. That's where the Vanguard oughta be." The Drifter's hand rests casually on the handle of a thick, breechloaded grenade launcher. "And ain't you Vanguard through and through these days?"

Joxer snorts at the irony. "I'm not here to hassle you, Drifter. On the contrary. Consider this a friendly warning."

"Friendly, huh? Is that what we are now?" Drifter's grip on the grenade launcher tightens. "Now you raised my suspicion. You better speak plain, Joxer, or prepare to draw."

The Titan shakes his head in exasperation. "Some people say those Pyramids damn near wiped us out once. Nobody knows for sure. But if they do end up hostile, it's going to get heavy in a hurry. And you don't want to be the guy standing in the middle holding a bag of Dark Motes."

"And what the hell business is it of yours where I'm standing?" the Drifter asks as he plants his boots on the deck. He rises to his feet, the grenade launcher dangling from his hand. "Unless I'm standing in your way."

Joxer puts his hands up in mock surrender. "You know what? I came here because I'm trying to change. Making amends. After what happed at Gambit Prime... I had to get right. And part of that is giving you some friendly advice to lay low for a while." He glances down at the Dark Motes. "But if you don't want to hear reason, that's on you."

Joxer trundles his way to the back of the ship. As the airlock hisses open, Drifter calls out, "That's real nice armor, Joxer. Don't forget where you got it."

Season 12

BEYOND LIGHT – SEASON OF THE HUNT

Humanity's ancient foe has returned. As the Black Fleet fills the sky, a strange power pulls friend and foe alike to the ruins of Europa, and a new Kell wields the gift of Darkness to unite the Fallen.

CLOUDSTRIKE

They return to moons devoid. Their eyes searching. It's just begun. Meet this storm of sound and fury, till thunder clashes fade to silence.

"Tell us about the Stormherd!" Kellikin shouted.

She resisted the urge to shush him because he'd been helpful earlier, yelling a warning to her when he saw the violet haze rising from the hilltops. It had given her time to call them into the bunker. Eldest of the children, he'd already experienced several voltaic squalls.

"OK. Gather round. Come on. Huddle up so I don't have to shout.

"A long time ago, the raiders came every winter. They came and took nearly all our stored food, and many in our village starved. But then spring would come with time for planting, and another summer. In the autumn, we harvested as we are doing now. Each time, we stored even more food, and we hid it more carefully, in case the raiders returned.

"And they did. When they saw that we had survived the winter, they fought even harder for our food, and found nearly all that we had hidden. And so it was, for too many years. They always took from us, never giving anything in return.

"And then, one autumn night, there was a great rumbling. At first some thought it was thunder, but it was the roar of the raiders' quads in the valleys. They had come early!

"Maybe they had a new leader. Perhaps they were too impatient for the harvest. We'll never know.

"Because as the raiders roared through our village, a blue-white bolt of lightning struck among them— BOOM! Before anyone's eyes had cleared of spots, a masked stranger clad in robes and wielding a crook had killed a score of them. With her weapon, she hooked lightning from the clouds and hurled it, thundering among them.

"They say there was something more than mortal about her, for those who were there said she could move faster than the eye could track, and her steps took her higher than anyone could leap. But eventually, the raiders surrounded her, and she fell to their guns.

"Yet there was something else different about her: the storm crow. It flew at her shoulder, and when she fell, it looked upon her body, and under its gaze, she rose again.

"This time, she pointed her crook to the sky, and clouds moved at her command. Our people fled as thunderbolts stampeded through the village. Our homes were not safe. Only our root cellars, like this bunker, were a refuge.

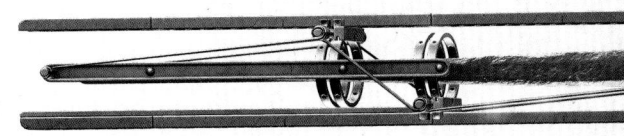

"No one emerged until the thunder ceased rolling. The raiders had fallen or fled. None would return, not until three winters had passed. And now, raiders only trouble us outside the village.

"So when you see the purple mist rise from the hills and hear the thunder, that is your sign to take shelter. And when you hear the rumbling roll through the village, it just might be the Stormherd, come back to make sure we're safe."

Thunder rolled again, but only a few children started. All looked to the ceiling and wondered.

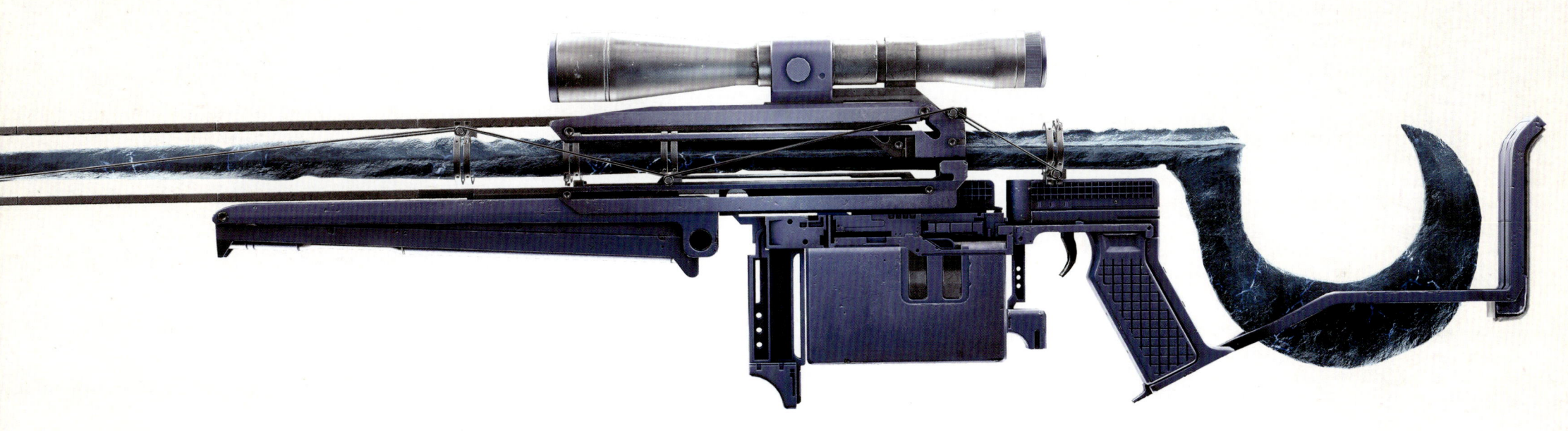

DUALITY

"The question becomes whether or not to fire, not where to aim." —Osiris

It was a trophy hunt.

One of Baron Spider's precious associates—the title he bestowed on those truly loyal to his cause—had vanished. Spider suspected treachery. He demanded Crow take to the field and come back with an answer—something Spider could use to encourage loyalty, he said. Something he could mount on his wall.

Crow had tracked the associate to an unexplored corner of the Tangled Shore, but when he finally crested the ridge, he saw exactly what he had expected.

The trail ended at a cryptolith, which jutted crudely from the dark basalt. The whispers of Xivu Arath had caught another of Spider's toadies—just like the last one, and the pair before that. But as Spider said, he wasn't interested in "mights and maybes." He demanded proof.

Crow knelt in the shadow of the cryptolith, the Lure already in his hands. There were recent Eliksni tracks in the fine blue sands; a dozen or so individuals. Nothing he couldn't handle.

He pulled a vial of condensed Ether from his belt and slotted it into the Lure. The concoction bubbled as it mixed with the soulfire inside the reservoir. Moisture beaded on the Lure's thin metal casing.

He drove the mount into a crack in the ground, adjusted the output, and watched as the thick pheromone mist rolled away from the Lure.

He waved Glint over and the pair headed to a rocky vantage point. He tinkered with the compression on his modified shotgun, placed it across his lap, and prepared himself for the worst part: listening to the cryptolith broadcast its malignant sermon.

He felt the presence of the spire itch on his skin. Crow tried not to stare at the grotesque totem as it twisted and hummed, but he felt profoundly uncomfortable when its pulsing light was out of his sight. It was as if he was being hunted.

Crow adjusted his weapon sights again as his silent vigil continued. He felt the stress beginning to wear on him. Waves of throbbing pressure emanated from the tower. His eyes ached. He concentrated on his breathing.

Glint flew to a nearby boulder to scan an interesting patch of lichen and Crow closed his eyes, trying to quell the nausea building inside his head. Hushed whispers surrounded him. He felt as though something reached out and caressed his chest, just above his heart. The scent of perfume, soft and familiar…

"Crow," Glint said.

Crow's eyes snapped open. "I see them."

A group of Eliksni Wrathborn were approaching the Lure. One among them wore the telltale quills of the House of Spider. Their movements were uncoordinated but had the troubling strength granted by subservience to Xivu Arath.

"They're already gone," Crow said bitterly.

The Wrathborn came upon the cryptolith. They were distraught, ranting. Their fury was rising. They lifted their voices in harsh clicking speech and tore at the ground around the Lure with their otherworldly power.

One passed Crow's perch, and he could see it: cloudy eyes, slavering jaws, an aura of wrath shimmering around it like a heated haze. It charged toward the rest and its rhythmic howls of rage joined theirs.

"They're chanting," Glint whispered, his curiosity forcing him to peek at the growing horde. "The syntax is garbled, but I could translate—"

"Don't," Crow said. "Please."

He looked down the sights of his weapon and started his work.

HAWKMOON

Stalk thy prey and let loose thy talons upon the Darkness.

What is this feeling?

I did not ask for it. I do not understand it. I do not want it.

The Crow is so carefree in his ignorance. The bonfire's glow lights up his pale features and I am drawn to the hope in his gold eyes. Where is the despairing child I anticipated?

He drinks from an open bottle of wine, against the recommendation of his Ghost. The Guardian encourages him, and they are laughing. This celebration is maddening; neither has reason to be so jubilant. Their world is ending, and they thrash like dying creatures in the final light of collapsing stars. They do not seem to acknowledge the futility of their existence, the impermanence of it in the face of cosmic annihilation.

Now the Guardian is drinking, standing close to the fire. Their Ghost, too, encourages them not to partake. They poison themselves for the enjoyment of it.

I am reminded of my sisters. Of moments spent by lapping shores, gazing up at infinite stars full of possibilities and wonder. I am left yearning.

What is this feeling?

I do not understand it. I do not want it.

They are celebrating their victory over the Taken. The Crow is making a gun shape with his hand, swinging the nearly empty bottle of wine around in the other like a sword. The Guardian looks pensive, sitting on a rock by the fire, contemplating the secret they are keeping. The Crow notices, but tries not to show it. He wants the Guardian's spirits to be lifted. He wants to be supportive, so that they may share in their triumphs together.

As equals.

I am reminded of my home. I am reminded of the warmth of the sun and the embrace of my family. I am reminded of my father's face. I am reminded of everyone I betrayed. All the blood spilled in the name of immortality. The warmth of the sun burns me with its memory.

What is this feeling?

I do not want it.

The fire has nearly died. The Crow fell over and cannot stand, though he insists he is fine. The Guardian is turning the embers with the tip of their sword. The Ghosts are talking to one another in quiet conspiracy. The celebration has ended, but I can sense their emotions are mixed: complex and myriad things, when a simple, singular focus would suffice.

There is a growing kinship here. Against better judgment.

What is this feeling?

EYES OF TOMORROW

"I want to see it all, unhindered, and know it's mine to take." —Clovis Bray

RECORD: Security Log E.P. Station, MTRLv2.18

IDENTITIES: C. Bray I, M. Liu

TEST SUBJECT: Sgt. Traore

FILE//DSC_CLASSIFIED

[M.L.] Test subject successfully through the portal. Direct feed is live. Multiple hostiles detected.

[C.B.] There are . . . so many of them.

[M.L.] The Vex numbers are incalculable currently.

[C.B.] Well, what are we waiting for? Launch the artillery.

[M.L.] Targets acquired. \<Weapons free.\>

[C.B.] How many targets are being tracked?

[M.L.] Four.

[C.B.] That's not enough. Fire now.

[M.L.] \<Fire.\> Test subject is under heavy resistance. Exo chassis receiving heavy damage.

[C.B.] FIRE. NOW.

[M.L.] \<Fire.\> Projectiles 1 and 2 dispatched. Two confirmed hits. Sir, the Torch Hammers are melting Sgt. Traore. Request retrieval.

[C.B.] Denied. Fire 3 and 4.

[M.L.] \<Fire Sgt.\>The left arm has been severed. He's incapable of action. Request retrieval.

[C.B.] DENIED. Use the right arm. Where's the feed?!

[M.L.] Test subject offline. Feed lost.

[C.B.] For the love of—do you see the cost of hesitation? Of cowardice?

[M.L] . . .

[C.B.] No matter. This is the price of advancement. The test subject was able to target multiple threats successfully but was simply unable to execute commands fast enough. The next hurdle requires a mechanism capable of housing projectiles for simultaneous fire that's lightweight enough for individual operation.

[M.L.] I'll get this report to R&D ASAP.

[C.B.] Tell them I expect to see an operational prototype by week's end.

[M.L.] Copy. Requesting retrieval of the remains, sir.

[C.B.] Denied. I will not allow the facility to be compromised or our portal to be breached. We'll double our defenses here and continue to send Exos through to fight the Vex on their front until we get this right.

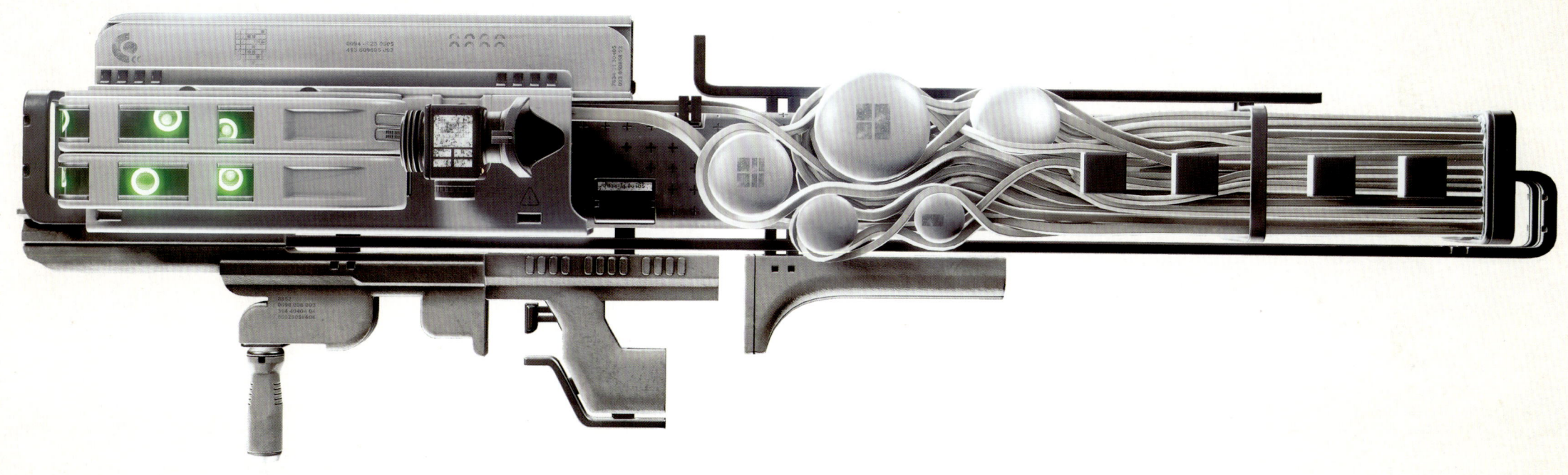

THE LAMENT

The last thing the Vex ever heard—the grinding wails of a vicious Banshee.

FROM THE DESK OF CLOVIS BRAY

Dear...me.

For one who has delved into some of the greatest secrets science has to offer, you would think I'd find speaking with oneself rather monotonous. However, this very letter represents a successful culmination of all I have worked to achieve.

You'll have questions, no doubt. Hopefully, by now, the AI has answered most of them.

Except one: Why?

Legacy, of course.

...Is the answer you'd expect from me. And rightfully so. It's not wrong, but it's only part of the story.

Frankly, I'm alarmed. For all my successes in scientific research, I have lacked any substantial findings of an afterlife. All I can find is death. An infinite nothingness. No remembering my loved ones, no seeing them again. No feeling their touch, or hearing their voices.

In my pursuit of eternity in this reality, I have foregone those niceties. Abandoned them. But you are a second chance. An opportunity to continue what I started and hopefully, in time, make amends with those I've wronged.

Attached to this letter, you will find a gift. A blade built just for you.

Keep it close. Never let anyone else take it. Stay alive.

For legacy.

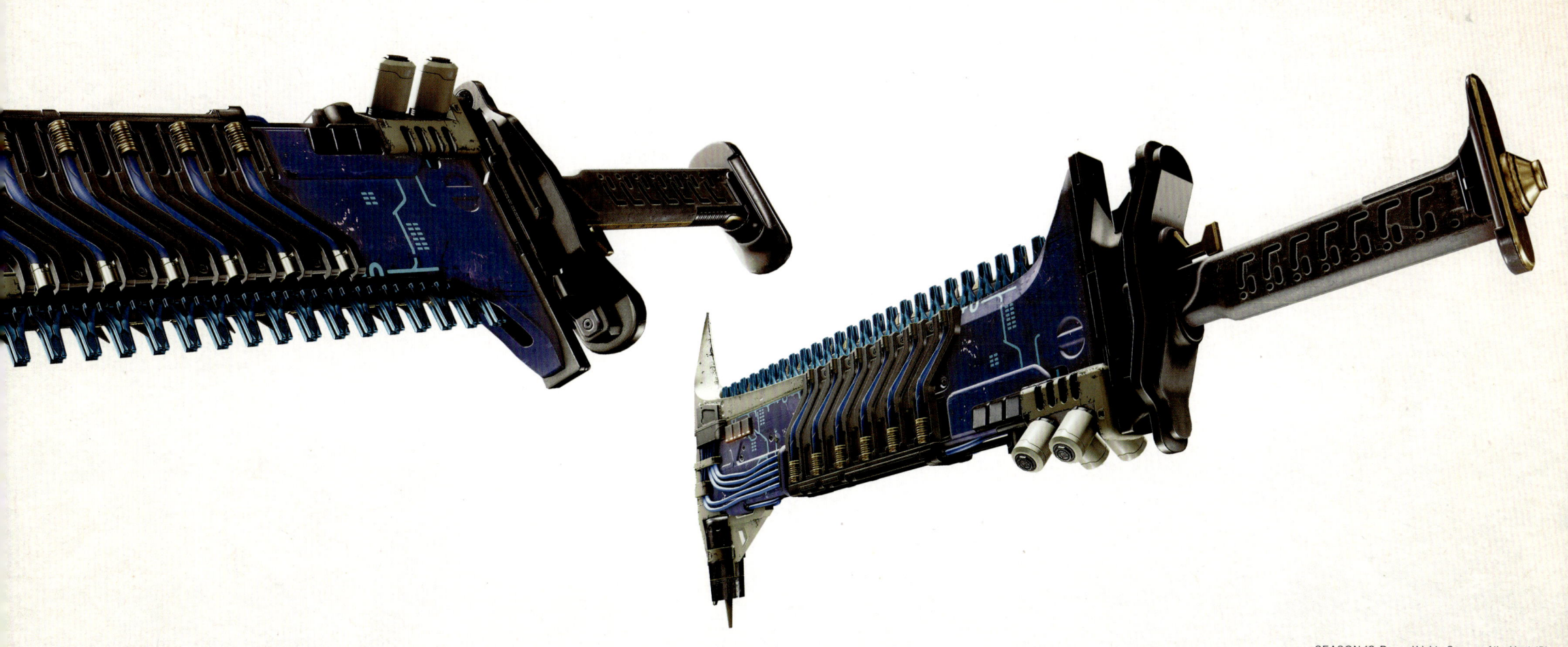

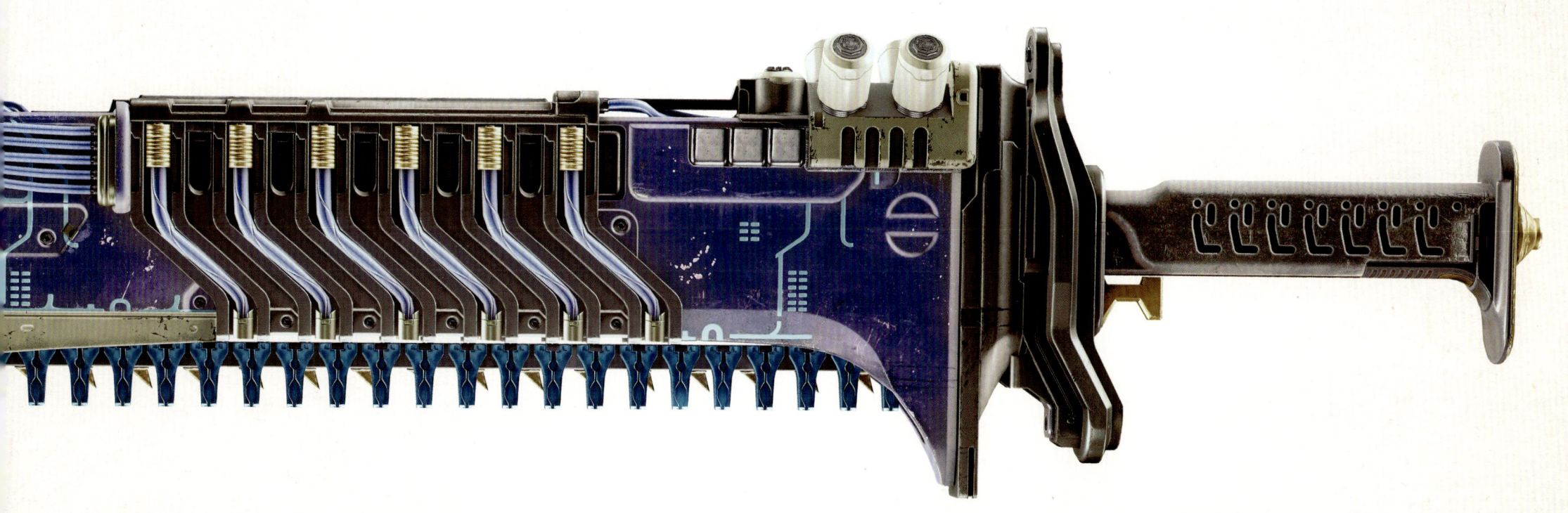

NO TIME TO EXPLAIN

A single word etched onto the inside of the weapon's casing: Now.

Novarro's timeline analysis indicates the weapon is the fabled Exo Stranger's rifle, enhanced at a future point in this continuity and then sent back to this present…

…on Europa. Late Golden Age. Deep inside a secret lab.

"Which window?"

"3025, Dr. Bray."

"I thought we'd run out of possibilities there?"

"We had… and then a new one popped up."

"Austen-1, how is that possible?"

"We don't know. We still don't understand how any of this works. It's highly volatile and uncontro—"

"Have we pinpointed the weapon's exact location?"

"More or less. Elsie-1 is supposed to attempt retrieval tonight."

"We can't risk the window closing before then. I'll be going this time."

"But last time, those things in the sky almost killed you."

"And now I know how they work. That's half the battle."

The old man gears up and enters a strange metallic pod made from Vex parts. Austen-1 stands at a distance from the pod, typing "April 10, 3025" into a console.

"All right, Dr. Bray. You're a go in 3…2…1…"

A burst of light.

An icy wasteland. What stood pristine moments prior is now dark, old, and falling apart, as if centuries have passed.

Clovis wades through the wreckage and comes to a frozen, deserted battlefield littered with Human, Exo, Vex, and alien bodies. He reaches down and brushes snow from one of the alien bodies, lifting one of its many arms.

"Fascinating…"

A piercing whir emanates from somewhere in the distance—Clovis looks up and sees a black and red ship floating in the air. It stops above the battlefield and emits a bright red light, scanning the area as if searching for something. Clovis slowly pulls a device from his pocket. He presses a green button, and the screen lights up, showing a blinking dot a few yards away. Very close to where the ship itself now searches.

He grabs a dead Exo and opens a panel on its arm, tinkering before closing it with care. He quickly sneaks away, and in seconds, the Exo explodes, drawing the attention of the ship. He sprints towards across the battlefield towards where it was searching only moments ago.

Using his device again, Clovis scans the ground until the blinking light goes solid. He digs into the snow until he hits something. He pulls it up halfway—a rifle, shining like new, etched only with one word: *Now.*

Clovis attempts to fully free the weapon. But it's stuck—attached to something. He pulls harder, revealing an entire dead Exo, hand wrapped tightly around the grip. He takes a good look at its face and gasps.

"Elisabeth…?"

The whirring sound reaches Clovis's ears again, pulling him out of his stupor. The ship heads right toward him. Clovis pries the gun from Elsie's rigid hand and sprints back the way he came, diving into his pod and activating it just as the ship fires on him.

A burst of light.

"You could have been killed," says a familiar voice.

"Instead, I got you a gift, Elisabeth," Clovis responds, catching his breath and dusting himself off.

"One down, an infinite number left to go. It better have been worth it." He looks into her eyes and musters a half-hearted smile.

"We'll make it so."

SALVATION'S GRIP

"I respect what I cannot steal from and you cannot take from the dark." —Excerpt from an old Eliksni salvage manifest

[In winding Eliksni script:] This power bestowed by the Dark was given first to the Eliksni—not to the machine-children, who are unlucky second-borns, unstoried and short in their memories. Just as the Great Machine touched the Eliksni first, so too does the Dark—though where the Great Machine's touch was fleeting, the Dark lingers.

[A scribbled note:] the cold Dark is an ENDLESS lingering

[In winding Eliksni script:] Encased in the cold Dark, you cease to be a flesh-and-blood thing but become a memory thing, a thing of stillness. To have memory is to be storied and to be storied is to be worthy, yes, but to be still is to be dead. We have not been still since the Long Drift, and we will never be still again.

[Scratched hard into the page:] stillness is more than weakness, it is NOTHINGNESS

[In winding Eliksni script:] Instead, we will make still and dead the things that seek to scratch out our memories, so they themselves will be dead-memories. We will mark this place as the Great Machine marked our home, and our story will be told in the scars we leave on this world.

—Notes on Stasis, or "the cold Dark," attr. to Kridis, trans. from Eliksni by Eris Morn

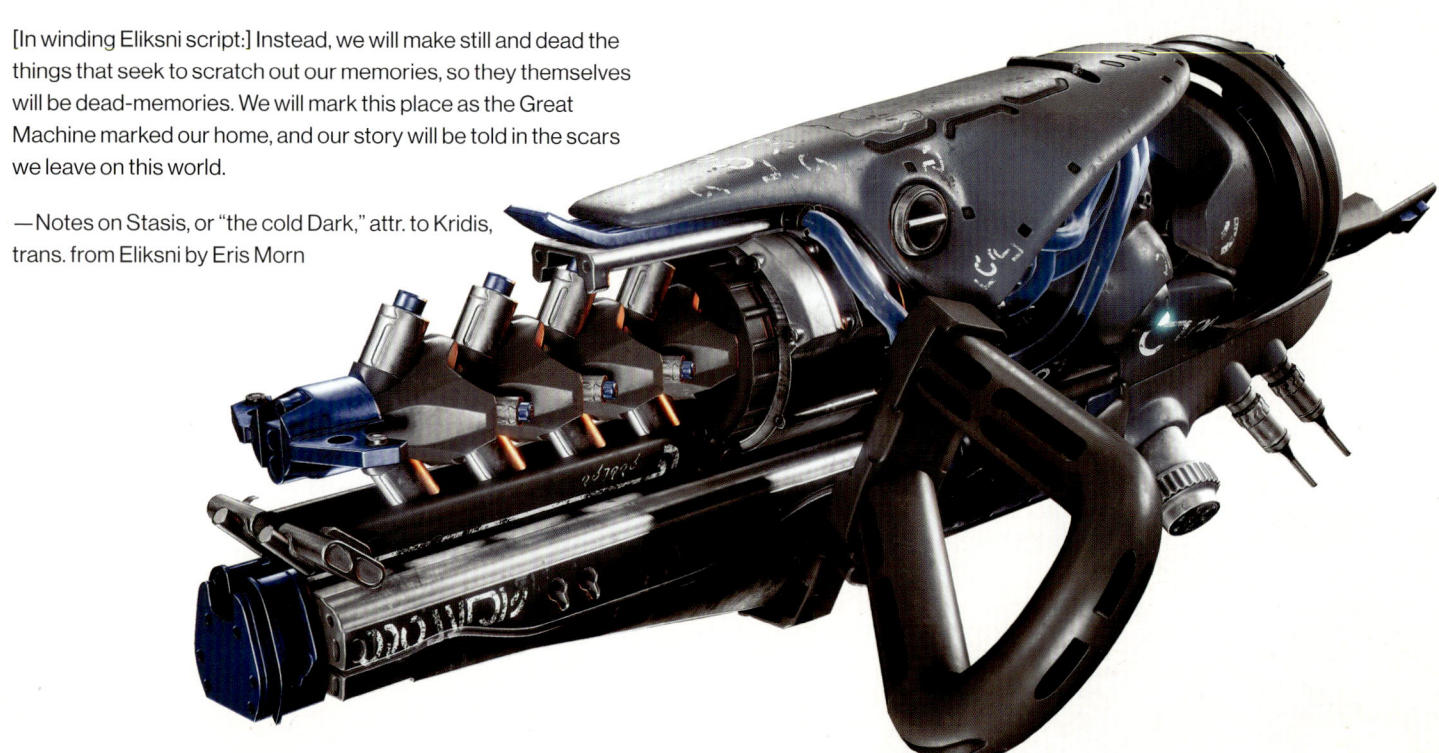

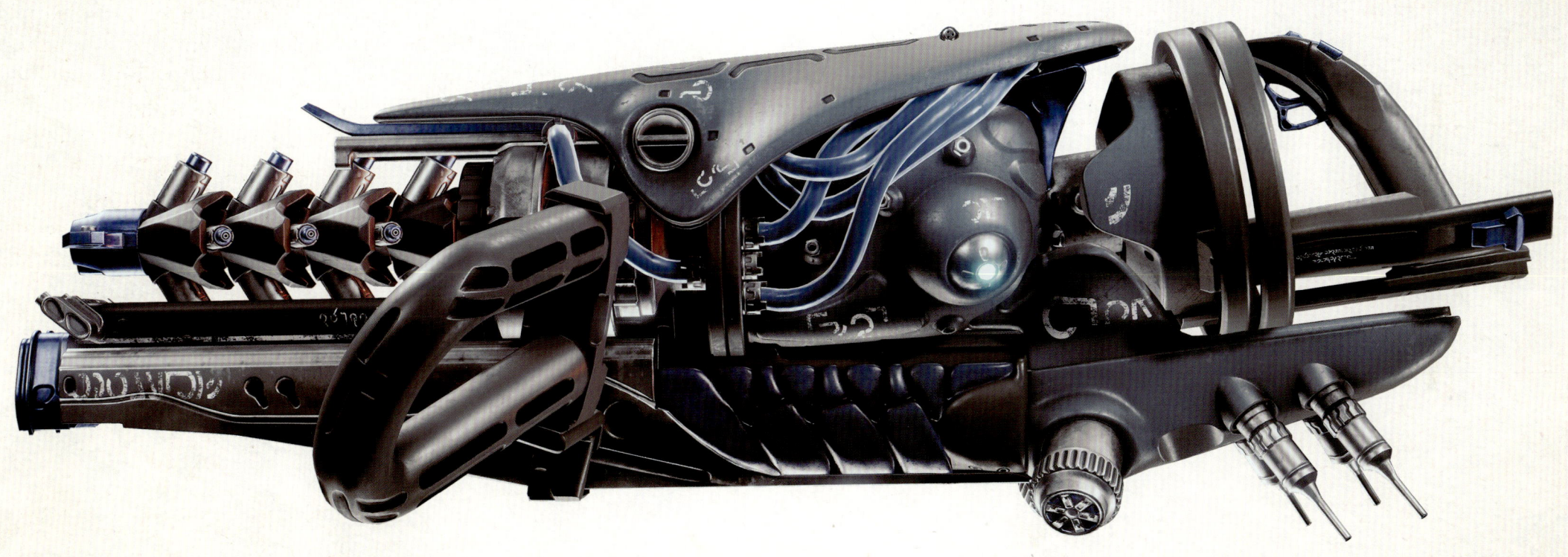

Season 13

SEASON OF THE CHOSEN

Caiatl, Empress of the Cabal, led her fleet to the Sol system and offered a deal to Zavala: Swear fealty, and defeat the Hive together. The commander refused.

The Guardian undermined Caiatl's attempts to form a war council, defeating her champions in ritual combat. Cabal renegades attempted to kill Zavala, but Crow foiled the plot, revealing his identity in the process. Zavala and Caiatl agreed on a truce.

DEAD MAN'S TALE

"Long, short, they all end the same way." —Katabasis

Gaelin-4's war beast leads us through balmy Venusian jungle. Our rifles low, our Ghosts high in the canopy like sentry drones.

"My vehicle is old. Needs maintenance. Been running too long without cutting the engine," I say.

Gaelin sends me a sideways look. "That shipwright still around? She used to make cider in the autumn. I swear, she kept us like a pack of strays."

I sigh. "No, I mean this thing." I run my hand over my body. "Besides, you know I can't go back there." I straighten the leather wrap around my Tex-foundry rifle.

"You know I literally tune myself, right?" asks the Exo Hunter.

"Why? You're immortal."

"And you're not?"

"I know, but I'm … slower. I feel slower."

"Uh huh."

"Just not like what I used to feel like. Not … spry. Not up here either." I tap my helmet.

"Tragedy. I feel for you. Have Gilgamesh tune you, then."

I chuckle. "Yeah … he'd love that."

"You two having issues again?"

I shake my head in a stiff, narrow lie. "You think we come back the same every time?"

"I do. Straight from the manufacturer," Gaelin-4 says.

"Sometimes I get the feeling … something's different."

Gaelin stops and squints at me.

I dip my head and let my hood fall forward. "Nothing I can put my finger on, just little things. Adjustments."

"You think he's changing you?" Gaelin's voice sounds more serious than surprised.

I wait too long to answer. It's not because I don't know my answer, but because I want to feel like I still doubt it. I raise my head. Gaelin meets my eyes and looks up to the canopy.

He leans his shoulder into me and drops his voice to a whisper. "My Clip's a good one, but you need to realize Ghosts don't know anything. Nobody does. They're just like us. They get curious. They question. If you think something's coming unwound, you need to sit down and talk it out."

"Wait … did Clip change yo—"

"Please," Gaelin scoffs. "You're paranoid." He turns to keep walking and calls back, "Life changes you. Same with them. I'm the only one that stays the same."

Gaelin raises a fist and we stop. His war beast sniffs the air and turns us east. We continue walking.

"What'd you name the beast?"

"Castus."

"You've been reading too many of the Spider's books."

"Some of 'em are good."

I laugh. "Aren't you the man that said anything you got tying you down can be made into a noose?"

"Yeah, some time ago."

"You've been taking a lot of jobs with him? Those Fallen?"

"You're one to talk, Emperor's lackey. Some of those Eliksni aren't so bad."

TICUU'S DIVINATION

Three points, pushed through forever.

The two Legionaries rooted through the armory of their deposed emperor. They swept the rubble aside and lifted a bow of sharp metal, its thin frame of blackened blades bound with wire.

"This is the one the Psions made so you can't miss."

"Huh. How'd they do it?"

"They put time in it."

"What kinds of time?"

"Kinds so when you shoot, that's always when the arrows hit."

"You never, ever miss?"

"Not unless you were going to anyway."

"But if you do miss, it'll make it a time that you don't?"

"Right. Unless this time was a time when you did."

**

It was the third day of the dry joining. Ticuu's voice was rasped raw, but still he clutched the bow to his chest and held it placid in his mind.

Ticuu melded his thoughts with the null. A bastardized metaconcert, one voice in the expanse—a temporal harmony of one.

Three arrows, hissing faintly with Solar power, bristled in his fist.

Then, an echo: a rusty whine of horsehair on frayed wire. Ticuu plucked the bowstring. Spots of blood appeared on the floor. He plucked again, filling the air with oppressive vibration.

Blood welled from his fingers and dripped to match the pattern at his feet.

**

"How's it make arrows?"

"They come from time, because they got put there before."

"When you shoot it, how's it know what heads to hit?"

"It goes in time and gets a future where heads always had arrows in 'em."

"But which heads, though?"

"The ones that had arrows already."

**

Ticuu's mind emptied itself, dissipating across the pitch and froth of what was to be.

Time was an empty wheel around him. His song held it, and the joining pinned it in place. Three points of harmony between the will and the physical.

His fist rose. Three shafts pierced his Y-shaped pupil. They had always been there. Three points, pushed through forever.

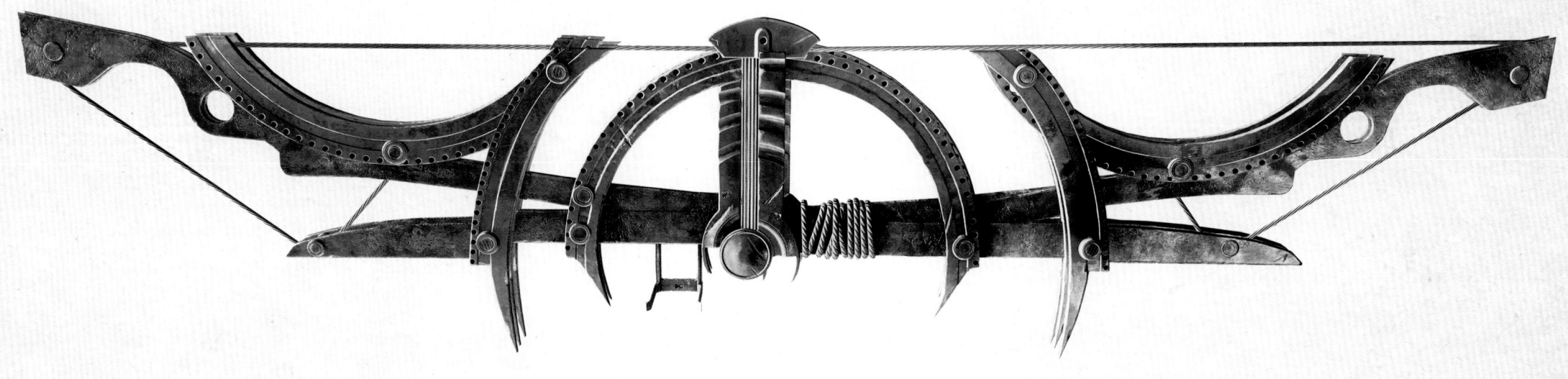

Season 14

SEASON OF THE SPLICER

As a Vex simulation plunged the Last City into darkness, the Vanguard turned to the Eliksni Splicer, Mithrax, for aid. In return, Ikora offered to shelter House Light within the City's walls—a controversial decision. With Mithrax's help, the Guardian learned to delve deep into the Vex network. There, they discovered the true mastermind behind the Endless Night: Quria, Blade Transform.

After defeating Quria, as well as a treasonous Vex invasion of the Last City led by faction leader Lakshmi-2, the Guardian successfully lifted the Endless Night. Mithrax and House Light remain in the Eliksni Quarter as allies of the Vanguard.

CRYOSTHESIA 77K

There are things colder than cold.

She crouched behind a sandstone boulder in the canyon basin and tried desperately to focus.

She clasped her lower hands together and squeezed. The feeling of pressure grounded her, made it possible to ignore the blood that flowed from the wound in her thorax. She could hear the Vex coming closer, their metal feet screeching against stone.

She raised her dominant hand and the thin spindles of her Splicer Gauntlet clacked into place and began to spin. She envisioned the Light surrounding—

She winced as weapons fire impacted the boulder at her back. Turned as it split apart, and for a moment, through the hot blowing sand and choking dust, she faced down an army.

She closed her eyes.

She saw the Vex targeting field sweep over her, flashing crimson and white. She shifted it with a wave of her hand and a hundred shots flew wide.

She felt dozens of Vex-shaped gaps appear in the air behind her and consolidated them. The Vex materialized in the same location and the fused metal mass fell heavily to the ground.

She looked over the gleaming field of enemies. The Light provides, she thought, and the next volley of Vex fire curved around her.

The Gauntlet on her wrist thrummed as a small portal opened in the air in front of her. She reached inside, felt the familiar shape of a short-term cortical conflux cube, and visualized crushing it in her hand.

A flash of light played over the red eyepieces of the Vex and they marched forward in lockstep, searching for a target they could not see.

She stepped to the side as they passed her.

As the last Minotaur stomped out of the canyon, she reached again into the portal. She willed their knowledge of Misraaks to her fingertips. She saw an image of his Skiff, flying low over the ice, framed in the minds of the Europan Vex. She pictured their awareness as a glass plane and envisioned it cracking, splintering into fragments of—

Inside the portal, dark threads wrapped around her wrist. She visualized them snapping as she struggled to withdraw her hand, but they stuck to her like pitch. She saw them crumbling under harsh Light, but the dust wet itself with her blood and dried around her hand. She saw the Light, but all she felt was the cold dark, freezing around her, holding her fast.

In the distance, the Vex turned as one.

VEX MYTHOCLAST

…a causal loop within the weapon's mechanism, suggesting that the firing process somehow binds space and time into…

Some legends live forever. Others are overwritten—reshaped by the sheer will of those who believe that any ordeal can be conquered, any foe vanquished, any god cast down.

The Mythoclast is a Vex instrument from some far-flung corner of time and space, mysteriously fit for Human hands. Its origins, mechanism of action, and ultimate purpose remain unknown. Perhaps it will reveal itself to you, in time…

SEASON 14: Season of the Splicer 171

Season 15

SEASON OF THE LOST

After Saint-14, Crow, and the Guardian raced to the Dreaming City to confront Osiris, Savathûn revealed the truth: Months ago, she had assumed Osiris's identity, sowing distrust and chaos within the Vanguard and beyond. After a confrontation, the Witch Queen restored Crow's memories of his days as Uldren Sov.

Now faced with his past, Crow retreated into solitude.

Queen Mara Sov struck a bargain where, in exchange for being freed from her worm, Savathûn would reveal the secrets of the Darkness. Intent on lifting the curse from the Dreaming City, Mara planned to kill her nemesis, but just as the separation ceremony completed, Savathûn escaped, her whereabouts unknown.

AGER'S SCEPTER

"One day, you will mold the world to your liking, dear brother, as I always have." —QUEEN MARA SOV

Mara Sov watched her brother imitate a swooping bird as he entertained a semicircle of children. They flocked to him as if the stories he spun were confections.

Uldren lurched to his feet—his shadow casting a heroic pose against a canopy of towering Baryon trees—and thrust a slender blade into the air.

"Straight through the storm!" he howled as Awoken children shrieked with laughter and applause. "That's right. The two kestrels were like blades sailing on the wind," he said, sheathing the fine steel. "As long as they were together, nothing could stop them."

Mara turned to survey the Awoken flotilla anchored deep within their borders, suspended around a floating starport. Soon they would disembark. This night was for revelry. For families to enshrine in their memories should loved ones fail to return. In the morning, Saturn waited.

Far-off asteroids groaned like thunder, sending the children into a frenzy of gasps.

"Sounds like Ager's having another battle," Uldren said, stepping onto a bench to get a better view. He brought a hand to his brow, as if sighting an advancing stormfront.

A young Awoken child, no older than six, stood. Uldren watched the worry well in her eyes.

"Is he OK? Can you see them fighting?"

"Oh, yes," Uldren answered. "Come here."

The child stepped forward.

"If I'm not mistaken, your name is Erith, isn't it?" Uldren asked. The girl nodded, awestruck. Uldren pulled a looking glass from his belt and placed it in her hand. "Look where I'm pointing."

Erith followed the prince's direction to a spot in the sky that flashed with color.

"I see Ager!" she proclaimed proudly. "I see Rega!"

Uldren patted her shoulder and smiled. "As long as the two of them are together, nothing can stop them. Just like us. Stand with your cousins, and you'll be all right."

Mara met his eyes and stepped forward. "That's enough. The prince has a long journey in the morning, and he must rest. Run along now."

Once the children were beyond eyesight, Mara's expression shifted to a glare. "These stories . . ." She leaned into Uldren. "Stop filling their heads with nonsense."

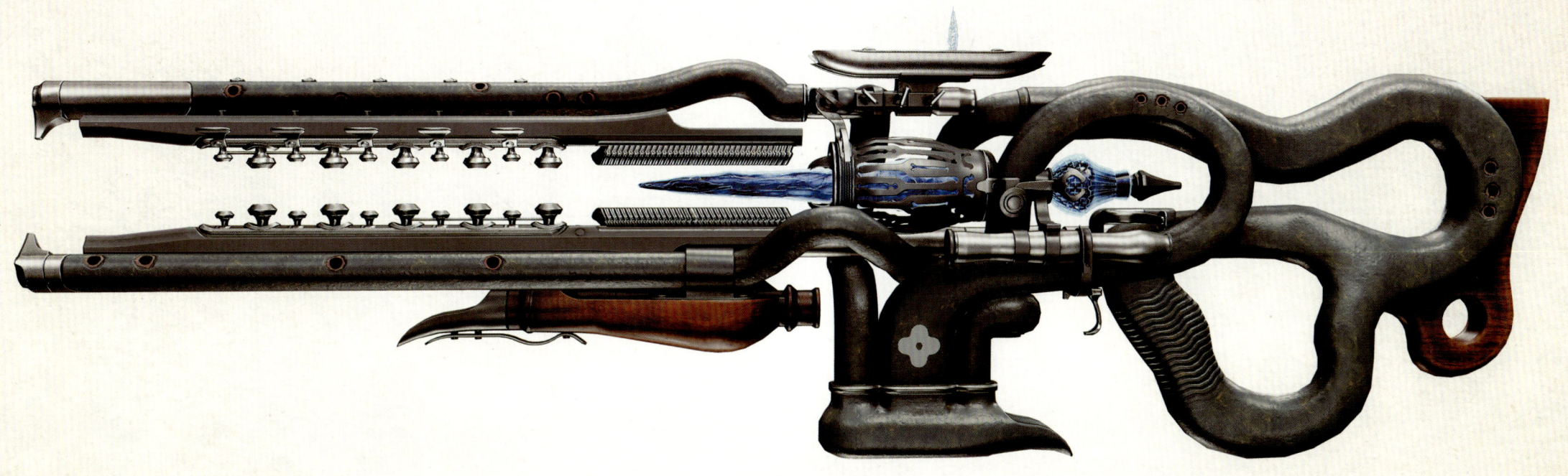

LORENTZ DRIVER

"Weapon system no longer explodes when trigger is pulled." —Prototype 7.2.1 Revision Notes

"What about this rifle?" Skorso asks over the sound of two Brigs moving cargo. Her overseer, a three-armed Vandal named Piiksi, pulls back the drop cloth covering it. He takes a moment to assess the way the rifle is pieced together from nonweapon components, then motions toward where the Brigs are walking.

"Good meals can still spoil," Piiksi says. "Bring it. But all these spare parts can be left behind."

Skorso nods in acknowledgment, but instead of immediately returning to work, she sidles up close to Piiksi, her eyes darting around the warehouse. "Is this really happening?" she asks in a whisper.

Piiksi steps away from her as she sets the rifle down on a nearby crate. "Maybe. Two hands in greeting, two hands concealed. It is a matter of survival."

Skorso challenges Piiksi's avoidance and circles around the crate, four eyes narrowed. "Spider's scared," she whispers again. "Isn't he?"

Piiksi quickly leans in. "You say that any louder, and I can't protect you from what will happen next," he says in a sharp whisper, glancing over his shoulder.

"Where would we even go?" Skorso asks, searching Piiksi's many eyes. Her supervisor's answer is a backpedaling shrug.

"Don't know," Piiksi lies and gives her a toothy smile. "But like some Eliksni say, the Light provides."

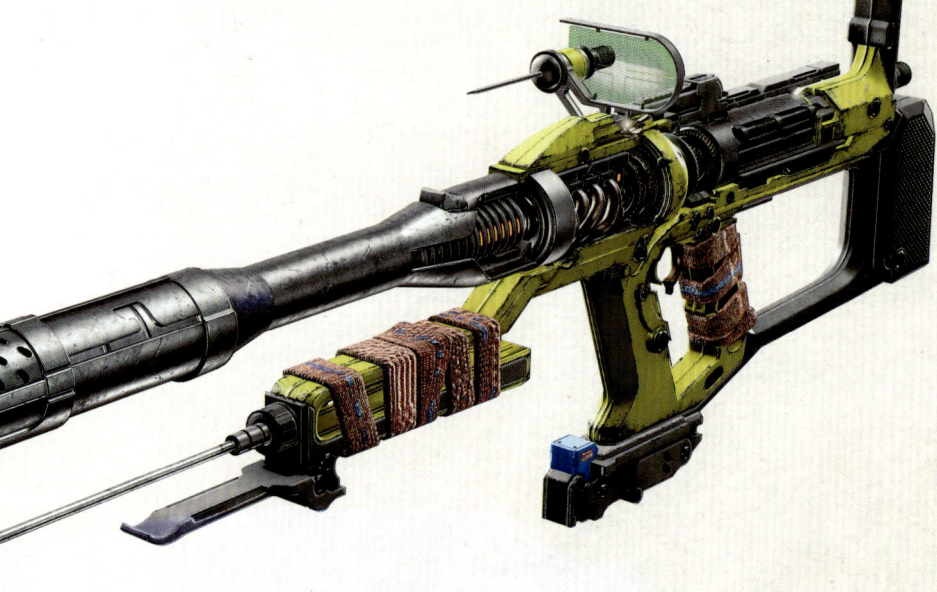

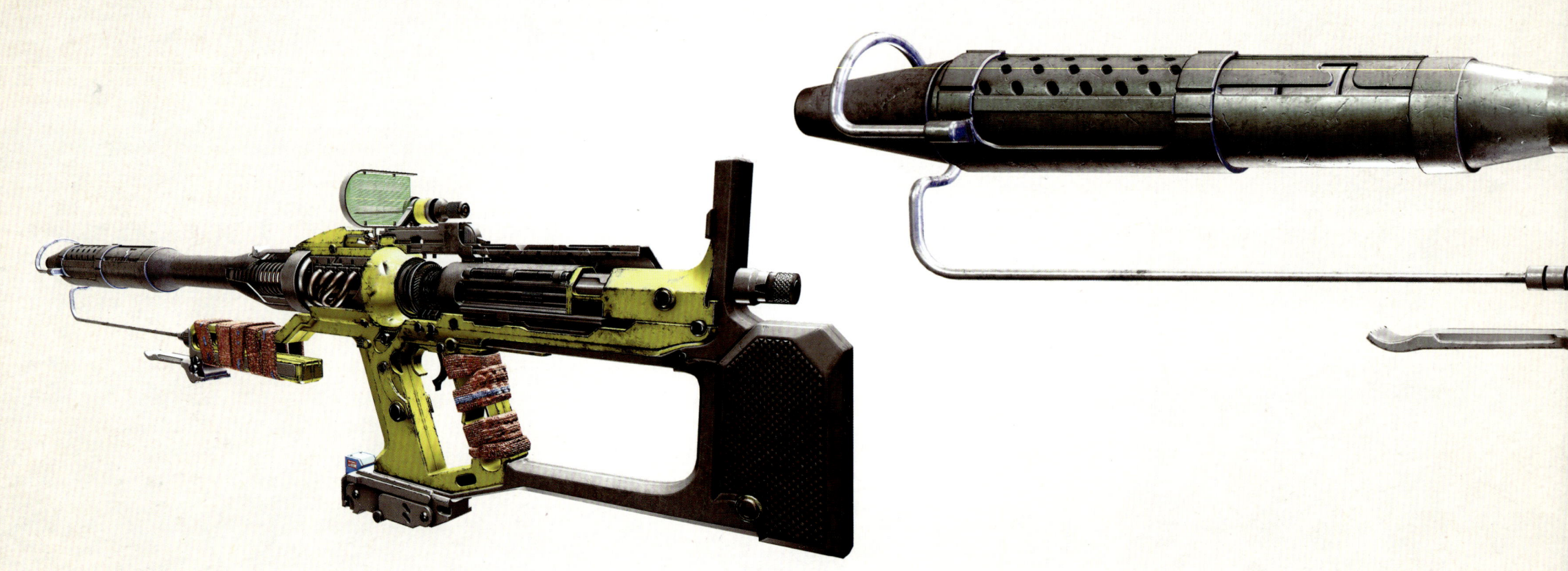

TITAN BOOKS

144 Southwark Street
London SE1 0UP
www.titanbooks.com

Find us on Facebook: www.facebook.com/TitanBooks
Follow us on Twitter: @titanbooks

© 2022 Bungie, Inc. All rights reserved. Destiny, Bungie, and the Bungie logo are trademarks of Bungie, Inc. in the US and other countries.

Published by Titan Books, London, in 2022.

No part of this publication may be reproduced, stored in a retrieval system, or transmitted, in any form or by any means without the prior written permission of the publisher, nor be otherwise circulated in any form of binding or cover other than that in which it is published and without a similar condition being imposed on the subsequent purchaser.

A CIP catalogue record for this title is available from the British Library.

ISBN: 9781803363462

Publisher: Raoul Goff
VP of Licensing and Partnerships: Vanessa Lopez
VP of Creative: Chrissy Kwasnik
VP of Manufacturing: Alix Nicholaeff
VP, Editorial Director: Vicki Jaeger
Designer: Monique Narboneta Zosa
Managing Editor: Maria Spano
Senior Editor: Jennifer Sims
Associate Editor: Harrison Tunggal
Senior Production Editor: Elaine Ou
Senior Production Manager: Greg Steffen
Senior Production Manager, Subsidiary Rights: Lina s Palma-Temeña

Insight Editions, in association with Roots of Peace, will plant two trees for each tree used in the manufacturing of this book. Roots of Peace is an internationally renowned humanitarian organization dedicated to eradicating land mines worldwide and converting war-torn lands into productive farms and wildlife habitats. Roots of Peace will plant two million fruit and nut trees in Afghanistan and provide farmers there with the skills and support necessary for sustainable land use.

Manufactured in China by Insight Editions

10 9 8 7 6 5 4 3 2 1

Based and built on the inspiring work of the talented individuals at Bungie—too numerous to note—who have each contributed in their own unique and important ways.

SPECIAL THANKS TO

Miki Bishop
Joseph Biwald
Allie Eibeler
Benjamin Fuhrman
Nutty Gettel
Tim Hernandez
Chris Hausermann

Katie Lennox
Ben Litowitz
Lorraine McLees
Garrett Morlan
James O'Donnell
Kevin O'Hara
Laura Scott